What Hope Looks Like

WHAT
HOPE
LOOKS
LIKE

1985

2009

*Use Your Pain to Fuel
Your Purpose*

ERIC D. NEWMAN

LIONCREST
PUBLISHING

WHAT HOPE LOOKS LIKE

Use Your Pain to Fuel Your Purpose

ISBN   978-1-5445-2201-2 *Hardcover*
       978-1-5445-2200-5 *Paperback*
       978-1-5445-2202-9 *Ebook*

To my wife, Analisa. You inspire me and make me a better person. And to my amazing kids, Camryn and Braxton. You remind me every day that miracles are possible. I have been called many things in my life, but nothing compares to "husband" and "daddy."

To my parents, Dan and Donna, and my sister, Cheri. You have never given up on me, even when it was hard.

CONTENTS

"Here's to the crazy ones. The misfits. The rebels. The troublemakers. The round pegs in the square holes. The ones who see things differently. They're not fond of rules. And they have no respect for the status quo. You can quote them, disagree with them, glorify or vilify them. About the only thing you can't do is ignore them. Because they change things. They push the human race forward. And while some may see them as the crazy ones, we see genius. Because the people who are crazy enough to think they can change the world, are the ones who do."

—ROB SILTANEN

INTRODUCTION

People who go through life-changing hardships respond in one of two ways once they make it to the other side: they either throw their experience away, never to speak of it again, or they embrace it and use it to help others.

I've done both, and the second path is far more rewarding.

When I was three, my mom took me to the doctor for a routine checkup. Seventy-two hours later, I was in surgery having a large mass and more than half of my liver removed. Then the doctor delivered news that changed our lives forever: "Mr. and Mrs. Newman, I'm sorry to tell you this, but Eric has cancer." He gave me a less than 10 percent chance of surviving, but after spending two years fighting for my life, I showed no evidence of disease, and my family breathed a short-lived sigh of relief.

In a sad, crazy twist, cancer struck our family again a few years later when my cousin—my dad's sister's daughter—was diagnosed with leukemia. Like me, Shannon was the second child in her family, she was three years old at the time of diagnosis, and she went through treatment until the age of five and then showed no evidence of disease.

Fast-forward a few more years. My dad's brother's second child, Nicole, was diagnosed with an inoperable brain tumor when she was three years old. We ended up losing Nicole within two years, when she was five.

Eight years later, Shannon's leukemia returned with a vengeance, and she lost her battle at the age of seventeen. Three cousins, all second born, all three years old when diagnosed, and now there was only one. Me.

As I stood in the freezing cold on the day we laid Shannon to rest, I couldn't wrap my head around why I was standing at the grave site of yet another young family member taken out by cancer. Then I was struck by a terrifying thought: *The cancer is going to come back and get me.* I suddenly felt like I was living on borrowed time. Rather than turn to my family and faith, I ran. I stopped talking about cancer. I stopped praying. I stopped reaching out to the people who cared about me the most. Instead, I began working hard, playing hard, and partying harder.

Over the next eight years, I started a couple businesses in lawn care and construction, made some real estate investments, and traveled and surfed all over the world. And did I mention I partied hard? I chased everything the world had to offer, and I succeeded in getting a lot of it.

Then in 2008 the economy took a horrible turn, and I lost everything that I had been chasing. In a matter of months, my life became a bad country song, the type that wins multiple Grammys. I lost my construction company, my fiancée, and my trucks—everything. I was extremely close to filing for bankruptcy, and I even had to move back home with Mom and Dad.

With $1,500 to my name, I did what any responsible twenty-six-year-old businessman living with his parents would do: I emptied my bank account and flew to Costa Rica.

I had all the essentials: bathing suit; faded, holey T-shirts; surfboard; and sunscreen. I even packed a journal, even though I had never journaled in my life. I spent my days in Costa Rica surfing, hiking, rock climbing, and otherwise avoiding the pain and fear inside. At night, when it was still and quiet, the thoughts would come roaring back as I rocked in my hammock. I had never felt so alone, so homesick, and so scared in my entire life. Several nights in a row, I opened my journal to write, but all I could do was stare at the blank pages, unable to convince my hand to put down a single word.

Then one evening, I prayed to God for the first time in years. Actually, I yelled at Him. "God, what the hell is going on? You got the wrong one! Shannon was so much better than me. Why am I still alive? What did I beat cancer to do? There's gotta be more to life than this!"

After I prayed and wrestled with God (it's okay, He can handle it), I turned to the middle of my journal and wrote one word: *hope*. I didn't write anything else. Every night I kept coming back to my journal, to that single word. I just kept circling the word *hope* over and over until I almost blew a hole in the page.

When I was growing up, my dad constantly reminded me that I was a Newman, that Newmans are strong, Newmans are courageous, Newmans are smart, and Newmans don't quit. At the end of every Newman chant, he would lean down and whisper in my ear, "And if you can beat cancer, you can do anything in this world."

One night while swaying and thinking, I remembered my dad's words. I had no idea what the word *hope* meant or what I was supposed to do when I returned home, but I was a Newman and Newmans never quit. I was broke but not broken.

A couple months later, someone asked me to help throw a fundraiser for our local children's hospital, the same hospital that saved my life many years before. As a cancer survivor, I had the opportunity to present one of those massive cardboard checks to the oncology floor. I was a little nervous about going back to the place where I had received treatment, but decided to push through the fear.

While I sat in one of those child-size chairs waiting to present the check, I suddenly heard an awful noise, like a grocery cart with a really bad wheel. I looked up to see a three-year-old kid, bald as a cue ball, rounding the corner as fast as he could. His mom appeared right behind him, pushing the screeching IV pole that was attached to her son and trying to keep up. The boy stopped right in front of me, looked me up and down, and asked, "Whatcha doing?"

I don't know what came over me. I hadn't talked about cancer since Shannon died eight years earlier, but suddenly I found myself telling the boy's mom the short version of my story. When I was done, she had tears in her eyes. "Wait right there," she said. "I have to get my husband."

I didn't want to wait. I had just made this lady cry, and now she was going to get her husband. No, thank you! But

I couldn't move. It was like my legs and feet were frozen. When her husband showed up, the woman said, "Tell him what you just told me."

So I did.

This time, Mom and Dad were both crying, and when I finished, the woman spoke the words that altered my life forever: "Eric, looking at you gives me and my husband hope that our son will be sitting in your seat one day, cancer-free."

Hope. That word hit me hard. As soon as she said it, something clicked. I remembered the word in my journal. Hope found me again. At the time, I was as lost as they come. I never dreamed I could give someone else hope. Instantly, I knew that I wanted to create moments like this for other moms and dads dealing with their child having cancer.

Exactly how I was supposed to do that became clear a couple months later.

I had been picking up odd jobs to pay the bills, and one day, my buddy Keith called.

"Hey, man, I've got a job for you. My wife is on me about building a playset. My kids are about to mutiny against me. Please, I'll give you four hundred bucks if you just come build this thing."

I needed the cash, so I said yes and I recruited my dad to help me. After all, I could only afford free labor.

When I arrived, I found that the playset had been left outside for six months. The numbers and coding had all worn off, making it impossible to tell which piece fit where, and the thousand nuts and screws had all been dumped into one bowl. I appreciated the job, but I wanted to give Keith a good ole roundhouse kick to the head. *Thanks a lot, buddy*, I thought.

A couple hours and three gallons of sweat later, I growled at my dad, "I quit. This is not worth four hundred bucks."

"You can't leave," my dad said. He nodded toward the house. "Look over there."

When I turned around, I saw the eyes, nose, and blonde hair of a little girl peeking out from the bottom of a window.

"She's been there for two hours," my dad said. "I'll pay you more. Just don't quit on that little girl."

Reluctantly, I went back to building, cussing the entire

time. I can frame houses and pour concrete, but nothing has kicked my butt like building that playset.

Twenty-one hours later, we finally finished. As I was putting the last anchor in place, I told my dad, "That is the last time I will *ever* build a playset."

Just then, the little girl busted out the back door, ran up to me, and gave me a giant bear hug. She stepped back, looked me straight in the eyes, and said, "Thank you for letting me play."

After witnessing the pure joy of Keith's daughter receiving her very own playset, I was reminded of the little boy at the hospital. He was full of energy and wanted to play, but many days he was restricted by the walls of the hospital and infusion IV poles. I turned to my dad with tears in my eyes and said, "What if...I'm supposed to combine the two major tragedies in my life, pediatric cancer and construction? What if I'm supposed to build playsets for kids fighting cancer?"

The one thing you never have to teach a child to do is how to play, and play is often the first thing to be taken from a child fighting cancer. I know that firsthand. My cousin Nicole was so swollen from radiation that she had to roll from one place to another. Because of her low immune system, it wasn't safe for her to play with the rest of us. She had to sit on the back porch and watch.

No child should have cancer, period. They sure as heck should not lose out on the one thing that they can never get back—their childhood. Play is the backbone of being a child.

Roc Solid Foundation began that day, in my buddy's backyard. That's where I caught a glimpse of how I could take my pain and turn it into my purpose.

THE POWER IS IN THE DECISION

Whether your life-changing struggle is cancer, abuse, homelessness, addiction, or anything else, like me you will be faced with a choice one day: throw away your experience or embrace it, show the world your scars, and take a stand to love and serve that community.

This book is for the second group.

Maybe you're at a decision point right now. Perhaps you've recently emerged from a tragedy, and you're tempted to put it behind you and move on. I understand that. I've been there.

At the same time, you might have the nagging sense that

you could do something with that experience to help others in the same spot where you once found yourself. Maybe you even have an idea of how you'd go about it, an idea that's your last thought at night and your first thought in the morning. If so, you might be reluctant to move forward because you know doing so will involve reliving old wounds.

I'm not going to lie. It will hurt. But what if you still said yes to digging deep into that pain so you could help others? What if you used that pain to fuel your purpose?

Possibly you are hesitant to move forward because you don't know where to begin. You might be wondering, *Do I start a nonprofit or a business? Where will I get the money? Will people understand or support what I'm trying to do? What if it fails? How will I juggle the time invest-ment with my full-time job?* Again, you're not alone. I have lived through every one of those scenarios and more.

When I started Roc Solid Foundation, I knew nothing about nonprofits. I had negative $750 in my bank account and no fundraising experience beyond selling Krispy Kreme donuts for my T-ball team when I was seven. When I pitched the playset idea to multiple people close to me, they pointed out various concerns: "You'll never be able to support a family." "You just failed miserably in your construction company." "Why can't you just go and get a normal job?" When I reached out to attorneys and accountants to file the incorporation paperwork, they thought I was crazy because (a) only millionaires start nonprofits and (b) we were in the middle of the worst economy since the Great Depression. Thank God I didn't listen to them.

Don't let today's fears dictate your decisions and stop you from making your idea a reality. I'm living proof that you don't have to be a millionaire, you don't need a fancy degree or sales or fundraising experience, and you don't have to be an expert in marketing or finance. If I can build a nonprofit from the ground up, so can you.

My goal is to keep the information I'm going to share with you clear and practical. I made plenty of mistakes, and I'm hoping to save you some heartache and headaches by gathering what I learned into this step-by-step guide.

In the pages that follow, you'll learn how to:

- Narrow down the problem or pain point and find your specific solution
- Set up the boring but crucial foundation: board of directors, legal matters, and finances
- Share your idea with others in a way that creates interest and gains momentum
- Create memorable and meaningful values to guide your decisions

- Attract and keep volunteers
- Fundraise creatively and effectively
- Avoid mission creep and stay committed to serving your primary audience
- Avoid founder's syndrome and learn to delegate
- Maintain your priorities so you don't lose focus on family...or your sanity

There's always someone walking into the gut-wrenching experience that you've walked out of. Having been in their shoes, you are in a unique position to solve a problem they're facing. With the tips, real-life examples, and resources provided in this book, you'll be able to use your pain to fuel your purpose and live for significance and success all at the same time.

WHAT HOPE LOOKS LIKE

About six months after I built the playset for Keith's daughter, I had a plan and I had my first cancer fighter to build for. Now I just needed the money. Since selling donuts was the only way I knew to fundraise, that's what I did. With the help of family and friends, we sold $3,500 worth of Krispy Kremes to fund that first playset.

The day of that build, the weather was not on our side, with rain and winds near hurricane force. By the time we finished, every volunteer was soaking wet, shivering, and exhausted. But none of that mattered when beautiful, bald Jillian came running around the corner and saw her playset for the first time, eyes wide and a huge smile on her face. Right then, we saw what hope looks like.

Hope is where your pain meets your purpose and you can visually see the solution. It's finding that tiny bit of light in a dark situation and moving in that direction. It's making a decision to focus on the good, even through devastating experiences. It's when the guy experiencing homelessness gets a job. It's when the gal dealing with addiction comes off drugs. It's when the family with credit trouble holds the keys to their first home. It's when the child fighting cancer is able to play. Hope is the result of turning your pain into your purpose.

Hope is the result of turning your pain into your purpose.

If you can walk through the struggle you've already experienced, there's nothing in the world you can't do. Picking up this book is the first step to changing your path *and* bringing hope to someone who desperately needs it. You may not be a Newman, but I know that you have what it takes to be courageous and not quit.

Ready to get started? Let's begin with getting your

thoughts on paper so you can figure out the problem and your solution. Someone out there is waiting for your idea!

Chapter 1

YOUR PAIN POINTS TO THE SOLUTION

When we were first starting Roc Solid Foundation, I had an opportunity to meet with the local children's hospital to pitch the idea of building playsets for kids fighting cancer. Hours before the meeting, I realized that we didn't have any marketing materials or brochures to leave after our big pitch. I ran to my computer, threw something together, and went to Office Max to print it out—and then noticed there were a ton of mistakes and the lettering was crooked. Hey, at least I had something.

I was extremely nervous, but I thought the meeting was going pretty well, until the head oncologist said, "Eric, this is a great idea, but how are you going to do it?"

At that moment, I had a decision to make: was I going to

BS my way through and act like I had it all figured out, the way I had in my recent failures in construction, or was I going to do things differently this time? This meeting was about more than me and making money. I'm sure I could have pretended, but this mission deserved complete transparency. Honesty is always your best bet, right?

"I don't know," I replied, looking down at the table. I slowly made eye contact, feeling like the meeting was gradually slipping through my fingers.

"Who's going to help you build these things?"

"I don't know that either."

"How are you going to pay for it?"

"I have no idea," I said, with a sinking feeling in my gut. "But if I can fight through the pain of cancer and losing my cousins, there is nothing in this world that I can't do or figure out."

What followed felt like the longest pause of my life. I thought the entire room could hear my heartbeat. Finally, the doctor looked at me and said, "All right. Let's give it a shot."

I was stoked to have our first hospital partner, but I

quickly realized this was a small win. Now I needed to get to work finding answers to all of the tough questions.

I had been so focused on my vision of helping kids with cancer that I hadn't figured out the who, what, when, where, why, and how to actually make it happen. The truth was, I didn't know where to start. I could read complicated blueprints and build a home, but this was completely out of my comfort zone. I pulled out my journal and wrote down the doctor's questions. Over the next few months, I started figuring out the answers, with the help of friends and Google, of course.

My goal in this chapter is to help you start off strong and get you to think through these questions *before* you find yourself in an important meeting, repeatedly answering, "I don't know." Preparation is key. You never have to recover from a good start.

Right now, you're probably feeling overwhelmed by the ideas, feelings, and possibilities swirling around in your brain. The first step is to get them out of your head and onto the page. Then you can start narrowing down the specific problem you're solving and the solution you're offering. You can also start organizing, prioritizing, and making a plan to turn your pain into your purpose.

You never have to recover from a good start.

BRAIN DUMP

As I said earlier, I wasn't much of a journal guy before my trip to Costa Rica. That's all changed. Now, I can't stop writing down my thoughts. You will never catch me without a journal in hand. I even keep a notepad beside my bed so I can write down the thoughts that keep me up at night, and then I transfer them to my journal. These regular brain dumps help me clear my head, stay focused, and make decisions that are best for Roc Solid and the community we're serving.

The process of writing your thoughts down is especially important right now, at the beginning of your journey. Action without aim is exhausting; just ask my son, Braxton. He loves Nerf guns and runs around the house like a Tasmanian devil shooting at nothing and everything, and then has to run back and find all the foam bullets he's sprayed everywhere. One day I found him out of ammo and lying on the floor, sweaty and exhausted from all his aimless shooting. (For the record, I have never seen a human sweat as much as my son.) If Braxton would have made a plan of attack and taken time to aim at his exact target, he would not have exhausted himself by chasing after all the bullets that missed the mark.

Action without aim is exhausting.

If you don't take the time up front to figure out the who, what, when, where, and why, you're going to wear yourself out like Braxton on a daily basis. Slow down, set your sight on your targets, and then take aim and fire. Even if you miss the target at first, at least you are still focused enough to take the shot and get close. Bad aim is better than no aim at all.

Doing a brain dump involves two simple steps.

STEP 1: GET A JOURNAL

Don't write ideas on random pieces of paper that you're sure to lose. Get a journal. I'm not talking about writing in your diary and hiding it under your bed or pillow. This is a simple and effective way to get your ideas organized and will allow you to start moving forward on the idea that has been keeping you up at night.

STEP 2: START WRITING

If you're not the journaling type, doing brain dumps might be awkward at first. You might stare at the page for a while, wondering what to write. That's okay; you're not alone. In Costa Rica, it took me an entire week to write one word!

If you find yourself staring at a blank page, start with something like, "Today, I ate ____." Write it fifteen times or until your hand gets tired. In the beginning, developing the habit of writing is more important than what you actually write.

The goal here is simply to empty that amazing brain of yours. Write down every thought that comes to mind in relation to your pain, the problem you want to solve, your solution, who might help you, what you might call your nonprofit, how you'll get money, how you'll tell people—anything and everything. If you also happen to think about your shopping list or the movie you watched last night or your upcoming vacation, write that down too. Just get it out of your head and onto the page. You might write twenty-seven pages, or you might write two—whatever it takes to get the ideas out of your head and into your journal.

Writing allows you to start busting through the barriers that might be stopping you before you even start. If you're wondering, "What if I lose my job? What if I can't pay my mortgage? Who is going to donate money?" write it down. Fears can be crippling. They can cause you to quit. By getting all of those worries out, you free up creative space to think through the problem and potential solutions.

In addition, the brain dump allows you to do some healing. As you write about the pain others are experiencing and how you're going to solve that problem, you'll probably feel your own pain. It's like bumping a wound that's scabbed over. Healing has taken place since the original injury, but there's still pain and possibly blood when the scab is disturbed. That's okay. Blood carries oxygen and proves there is still life coming from that wound. Revisiting old pain points will hurt, but it's important to capture those emotions. Let them fuel your passion to help others in the same place.

To give yourself a goal, set a timer for three or five or ten minutes. Writing doesn't feel as intimidating if you know you're only doing it for a set amount of time. There's a beginning and an ending, and you've automatically succeeded when the timer goes off. With every stroke of the pen, you are starting to solve the problem others are experiencing and creating change.

NARROW IT DOWN

After you have brain-dumped all of your thoughts, questions, fears, and feelings onto the page, sit back and take a look at what you have. Somewhere in those words lives *the* problem you were created to solve. It's *the* pain point you wished someone had taken the time to relieve, and even better, eradicate from the face of the earth.

You might not see it at first; you might have to dig a little deeper. Try this exercise: venture back to the time when you were actually going through the pain and start listing all the problems you experienced. As tough as it might be, try to revisit that time visually, mentally, and emotionally, and write down as many pain points as you can.

After you identify these problems, ask yourself, "If I could have had one thing that would have solved this problem, what would it be?" Write the answer (or answers) next to each problem you listed. That's your first attempt at a solution.

When you have a list of problems and potential solutions, you're ready to start narrowing it down. Look at the pain points and see if any of them can be grouped into "buckets" related to the same root problem. For example, if you are serving the homeless community, your buckets might be transportation, food, shelter, and healthcare. For me and the cancer community, the buckets may be play, physical therapy, family, or financial support. Placing ideas into buckets will help you organize your thoughts and narrow down the one problem you are trying to solve.

At times, you may list a problem that is actually a cause or effect of the true problem. For example, a person dealing with homelessness lives on the street. Being homeless is not the true problem, however; it's the result of something deeper. The person might be dealing with a mental illness that makes it hard for them to hold down a job. Not having a job limits their income, which in turn limits their ability to pay rent. Another problem could be that they don't have reliable transportation to and from work, which would again lead to lost jobs, lack of money, and an inability to pay for housing, all of which result in homelessness. The problem of mental illness would involve a different solution than the problem of unreliable transportation. It's important to get to the root cause in order to provide the correct solution.

If you're still having a hard time narrowing down the pain point, you might google the problems you've listed and look for pictures that suggest a solution. World problems like "homelessness" and "pediatric cancer" are too broad. Focus on one main point within that larger problem.

After you put in your search terms, scroll through the images. Look for problems that you may have faced and that ring true for you, as well as a smaller slice of that pain you can solve. Now look for pictures that suggest a solution that would have helped you at the time, as well as those who are experiencing that problem now. If something jumps out at you, find a way to get that picture in your journal—take a screenshot, print it, sketch it. In fact, feel free to put down this book and start googling right now!

When I searched for "kids with cancer," I noticed that none of the children were playing. They were all in hospital beds. I hardly saw any smiles. These images and my own experience led me to one specific pain point that wouldn't go away: a child with cancer loses out on play. I kept thinking of my cousin Nicole sitting on the back porch because she didn't have a safe place to play. That was the specific problem I wanted to solve, and my specific solution was building playsets. I wanted to give children the opportunity to play in the safety of their own backyard.

If an online search doesn't help you identify a specific problem and solution, try creating a mind map. Write each problem on a separate page and circle it. That's the hub. Draw lines coming out from the problem, and at the end of each "spoke," write a possible way to solve that problem. Now that you have them in front of you, start crossing "solutions" out until you have one or two to work with.

Narrowing down your specific problem and solution takes time. It probably won't happen overnight, so be patient and keep massaging your idea until you know exactly how you can bring hope to the community you were called to love and serve. This is the all-important first step. You must know the problem you're solving and the solution you're offering before you can figure out your program (Chapter 3) or get people to help you carry out that program (Chapter 5) or decide how you're going to fund it (Chapter 6).

PRIORITIZE AND TAKE ACTION

Another way to use the brain dump and mind map exercise is to organize and prioritize the things you need to do. Now we're going to start bringing order to the jumble of ideas.

After you narrow down your problem, write it in the center of a clean page of your journal, circle it, and draw lines out from it. This time, at the end of the spokes, write down thoughts related to that problem (pain point): questions, doubts, potential roadblocks, best-case scenario, worst-case scenario, things you might need to do, fears, hopes—anything and everything you can think of.

At this point, it might help to consider the doctor's questions that I couldn't answer. Add spokes to the hub with ideas related to the following:

- Who am I trying to help?
- What am I going to do for them?
- When am I going to do it?
- Why am I going to do it?
- How am I going to accomplish this?

The next step is to create your first to-do list using your brain dump list and your hub-and-spoke mind map.

I use a numbering system to prioritize what should be tackled first, second, and third. Number ones represent items that should be done immediately and must be completed before any other items. Number twos should be done in the next few days, and number threes can be done in the next week or even in the coming months. To keep the ball rolling, I tend to delegate the twos and threes.

After I assign my initial numbers, I take all the ones, move them to a separate page in my journal, and prioritize them. For example, deciding on a name for your nonprofit and buying a domain name are both number-one priorities; however, you have to pick a name before you can buy the domain. This list of prioritized number ones is your immediate-action list.

After you knock out your first action list, evaluate your number twos to see if any should be bumped up to top priority or possibly moved down to number three and delegated to someone else. Don't skip the twos! And, don't be scared to delegate your number twos or threes to others. Remember Braxton? Action without aim is exhausting. Having a prioritized list keeps you focused and gives you a target to aim at.

Now, you might be thinking, *How do I even know where to start? What are the priorities?* In general, the chapter topics appear in order of the actions you need to take; in other words, you'll want to address the items in Chapters 2-4 before you start thinking about, for example, fundraising (Chapter 6).

After reading each chapter, come back to your original brain dump list and add priority rankings—or create a whole new brain dump or mind map with the things you've learned from that chapter. The important thing is to get those swirling thoughts on paper, prioritize your tasks, and then take action.

NAMING YOUR NONPROFIT

When I was diagnosed with cancer, my dad bought me a Garfield stuffed animal and had my childhood nickname embroidered on the front: E-rock. Before I could even hold the toy, however, the nurse had Garfield sanitized. Stuffed animals carry a lot of germs and I was about to start chemotherapy, so we couldn't take any chances. When he came out of the washing machine, Garfield was clean, but he looked forty years old and ragged, and the *k* had fallen off my nickname.

Twenty-two years later, I was sitting in our world headquarters—the room over my parents' garage—trying to figure out what to call my new nonprofit, when I saw Garfield sitting on a shelf. I stood up and put my hand in front of the E and focused on the "roc." I started brainstorming and soon landed on the name we have today: Roc Solid Foundation.

Naming your organization is an important step. For one, naming something makes it harder to kill. Plus, if you don't have a name, you won't be able to move forward with the official paperwork discussed in Chapter 2.

Here are some tips for coming up with a name that is true to your mission, a list I wish I had when I first got started.

Use bold, descriptive words. The name should hint at an action or truth you want people to remember. Most people know the phrase *rock solid* or *solid as a rock* and think of strength, inner as well as outer. Kids fighting cancer are rock solid.

Make it easy to spell. If people can't remember how to spell it, then it's not simple enough. Yes, the "Roc" in Roc Solid breaks this rule, since people think there's a *k* on the end. We got lucky because the story of naming the nonprofit includes an explanation of the spelling. For example, whenever someone from our team talks to the media, they say something like, "It's R-o-c. The k fell off." I discuss another way around different spellings in the section on domains.

Make it easy to pronounce. You want people talking about your nonprofit, so make it easy to say. Over the last couple of years, I have interacted with a few nonprofits with missions that I love, but to this day I cannot pronounce their names. If the name is not easy to say, it will be easier for people to forget.

Make it short and sweet. I recommend keeping it to no more than twelve letters total. When you're writing an email, you don't want the name to take up the whole subject line because it's so long. Roc Solid Foundation is more than twelve letters, so we often shorten it to Roc Solid.

Make it unique. The sweetest sound to any human is their name. Likewise, the sweetest sound to any founder, board member, and volunteer should be the unique name of their nonprofit.

Try to keep your name out of it. Who started the Make-A-Wish Foundation? Most people couldn't tell you, but they do remember the nonprofit's name and what they do. They have a name worth remembering, one that points toward their mission of making wishes come true for children fighting a terminal disease. Create a name that's worth remembering, one that will outlive you and your personal name.

Make it easy to understand. As you consider ideas, ask yourself, "Who are we serving? Will they get this?" You want everyone to understand the name of your nonprofit, but most importantly, the community you're serving. It's more important to be clear than clever. You want the name to roll off the tongue.

Bring hope into the equation. I don't recommend naming your nonprofit in a way that focuses on the harsh reality of what you're doing: for example, the Rest in Peace Julie Foundation. You want to offer hope and light and put a positive spin on the pain point. One amazing family I know is starting a nonprofit to provide Lego sets in hospitals so children who are stuck in their rooms have something to do. They started this nonprofit in honor of their daughter, Kaylee, who loved Legos and lost her battle to cancer. The name Kaylee's Legocy puts a positive spin on the pain point and also communicates something about their mission.

Put yourself in your audience's shoes. Will they understand your purpose? Will they gain hope from your name?

Embody your mission. Later in the book, you'll hear about Jason, who started a nonprofit to provide suits and interview training to men living on the streets. He named his organization Get Suited, which clearly shows his purpose, his goal, and why his nonprofit exists.

Make-A-Wish has their mission right in the name. I wish I would have spent more time up front figuring out a name that shared our mission. Instead, we created a tagline: "Building hope for kids fighting cancer." If you can't do it in the name, do it in the tagline.

Make sure the domain is available. If you already have a list of names, put down this book and go research available domains. GoDaddy is one site where you can check availability, but there are others. Don't wait until after you choose a name to do this step. In today's digital world, a domain is essential, so include that research as part of your decision-making process.

I wish I would have searched and purchased the domain RockSolidFoundation.org and RockSolidFoundation.com as well as the spelling we use RocSolidFoundation.org—partly because if someone searches for Rock with a *k*, they would still be sent to our site and partly because RockSolidFoundation.com now belongs to a company that produces rap videos.

Nonprofits are typically.org, but I suggest you buy all of them if you can:.org,.com,.net, so if someone types in the wrong ending, they will be redirected to your site anyway.

NAMING YOUR NONPROFIT CHEAT SHEET

1. Brain dump.

2. Bucket your ideas.

3. Ask for genuine feedback from two people—ideally someone who is the artsy creative type and someone who can look at your ideas from a marketing or financial perspective.

4. Narrow down your ideas to two or three options.

5. Check the availability of domain names and social media handles.

6. Think through logo ideas, branding, and so on.

7. Decide and register.

Stay away from hyphens, underscores, and extensions in the domain name. For example, if Charity.com is already taken, don't take the domain Charity1.com or CharityLA.com just because it is available. Five or ten years down the road, the person who owns the name on which you added the extension might trademark that name, and then you'll be forced to change your nonprofit's name. That can be extremely detrimental to your organization and to you because rebranding is expensive. Take the time up front to figure out the best name. I'll say it again: the domain shouldn't be an afterthought. Include it as part of your decision-making process.

Check availability on all social media channels. That

means check Twitter, Instagram, YouTube, and so on. You want to speak with the same voice on every channel. If at all possible, all social media handles should be the same or as close as possible. It helps to add consistency throughout your brand.

Visualize the name as a logo. After you've checked the domain, take some time to visualize that name as a logo. What will it look like on your website? On a hat? On your business card? On marketing materials? This is where you also want to think about design and color scheme. If your logo has twenty-five different colors, it's going to be expensive to produce and more difficult to keep a consistent brand.

Many people skip the domain part and go straight to the logo. They decide what they're going to name their organization and immediately start working on branding and marketing materials. Once they check the domain and realize it's taken in every form, they have to start over. It's easy to get caught up in branding and marketing first because they are tangible, but the result can be a lot of wasted time and money.

After you've narrowed down your problem and solution and picked a name for your nonprofit, it's time to get unsexy. Yes, you read that right. There is nothing attractive or thrilling about laying the foundation of your organization, but it is essential if you want your dreams to turn into reality.

TIPS FOR THE FUTURE

Because of time and money, you won't be able to do everything right away, and that's okay. Here are two tips for the future related to your nonprofit name and logo:

1. Look into trademarking your name. You might not be able to afford it right now, but it's something to consider down the road.

2. When you find someone to help you design your logo, ask them for a brand standard kit, which will help you keep all of your logos looking the same, both now and years down the road.

Chapter 2

"THAT'S A SEXY FOUNDATION," SAID NO ONE, EVER

As the idea of building playsets began to spread, one of my dad's friends arranged for me to meet with a very successful CEO who did a lot of charitable work.

"Make sure you dress professionally," I was told. "Gary gets right to business and is one of the best-dressed guys in town."

I am a surfer, beach lover, and bathing-suit type of guy. I didn't even own a suit, so I borrowed one that ended up being two sizes too big. When I reached out to shake Gary's hand, the sleeve covered my knuckles and half my palm. My handshake was firm, but the sleeve in between our hands made me feel childish. I was horrified. In my mind, the meeting was over before it even started.

As soon as we sat down, Gary started firing off questions. I quickly realized he was not big on small talk.

"So, are you a 501(c)(3)?"

"A 501 what?" I asked, staring back at him like he had three heads.

"A nonprofit or charity. You are trying to become a philanthropist, right?" *Philanthropist?* I hadn't heard that term before and anything with an *-ist* at the end couldn't be good. Still, I wrote down 501(c)(3) in my journal.

"Do you have a board of directors?"

"No, sir." I wrote down the question.

"What kind of financial structure will you have?"

What the hell is a financial structure? I thought as I wrote down the question. At this point I was also thinking, *There's no way this guy is giving me any money.* I began to sweat in my oversized suit.

"Do you have a sustainability model? Are you incorporated? Do you have a marketing plan?" No, no, no...not even close.

"Eric, when you have these things, come find me." And just like that, the meeting was over. As I walked out the door, I imagined Gary hopping on the phone to call my dad's friend and tell him what a joke I was and that I had wasted his time. I felt humiliated.

Still, I went home and cleaned up my notes, excited to put a plan in motion to tackle Gary's questions. The only problem was, I had no idea where to start, so I started calling friends and family—anyone I thought might be able to guide me. Next I prioritized my tasks into what had to be done first, second, and third.

It took me about a year and a half, but I checked off every item on that list and laid a solid foundation for Roc Solid in the process. The only thing left to do was find Gary. I was so excited and nervous at the same time. What if he had forgotten about me? I tried calling him a couple of times, but he never responded. I stopped by his office, but he wasn't there. I worried that I really had blown that meeting, and I started to lose momentum.

Then one day, I picked up a local magazine, and there he was. Gary had won an award, and it was being presented to him at a nearby hotel and conference center.

So, I bought a ticket to the event and showed up in the same oversized suit. I quickly spotted him at the VIP table, front and center. I was sitting all the way in the back in the cheap seats.

I was there for one reason and one reason only: find Gary. As I was making my way up to his table, the music started playing and the program began. I didn't return to my seat; I was on a mission. I scrunched down and kept walking. The path across the room felt like a mile-long obstacle course, and I weaved in and out of tables and chairs, clumsily bumping into people along the way. When I finally got close, I stood up, straightened my oversized suit, and confidently walked over to him.

"Excuse me, Mr. Brandt," I said.

He turned around and said, "Well, Mr. Newman. I've been thinking about and praying for you since our meeting."

Squatting next to his table, I reached into my jacket pocket and pulled out the original checklist from our meeting. "I completed the tasks you gave me," I whispered. "You told me to come find you once I finished them. So, here I am."

He smiled. "Call my assistant on Monday and we will set another meeting."

I nodded and turned away, grinning from ear to ear. I felt like I had just scored the game-winning shot at the buzzer.

The big buckets in this chapter come from my conversation with Gary. They might be seen as absolutely boring and equally necessary, just like the foundation of a building. Over the past twenty-plus years, I've worked on every phase of construction, from beginning to end, and not once has anyone complimented the foundation of a home or office building. In a sense, that's crazy because the foundation is the most important part. The stability of the rest of the structure depends on having a solid foundation.

The same is true of your nonprofit. Along with narrowing down your pain point and solution, you have to set up a solid foundation before you can start building your program and the rest of your organization. Laying a solid foundation involves a lot of underground work, things most people will never see. It's the mundane part of construction, and it's the not-so-exciting part of building a nonprofit, too. If you skip this step, however, it is extremely probable that the whole thing will come crumbling down, and you will miss your opportunity to put your solution to work for those who need it.

By this point you are probably emotionally connected

with your problem and solution. I get that. All I wanted to do was turn my pain into my purpose and build playsets. I didn't want to think about financial systems, marketing, or sustainability. But the mission will only go so far if you don't lay the proper foundation and get organized. As I learned from my meeting with Gary, you have to get organized *first*. If you don't, your passion is going to slowly drain away as you tire yourself out by acting without aim. Having a solid foundation will guide your actions and help you make the best decisions now and for the future of your nonprofit.

If you're not a naturally organized person, this part might scare you a bit. The way I see it, you can either learn to be organized and lay a solid foundation or find yourself broke, in legal trouble, and unable to serve the community you want to serve. When you think about it that way, the choice to get this part right is pretty clear.

In this chapter we'll talk about three key areas that will make up the foundation of your nonprofit: board of directors, legal aspects, and finances.

BOARD OF DIRECTORS

After making my phone calls for help, I decided to start with Gary's question about having a board of directors.

BOARD OF DIRECTORS CHECKLIST

☐ You (the mission driver)

☐ Lawyer (the person to keep you out of legal trouble)

☐ Accountant (the person to keep the money straight)

☐ Marketing expert (the person to get the word out)

☐ Sales expert (the person to oversee development and fund-raising)

I had no idea who should sit on the board of a nonprofit, so I did some research online.

WHO SHOULD SIT ON YOUR BOARD

One thing I immediately noticed while scrolling through the internet was that almost every nonprofit included legal representation on their board, so I wrote down "lawyer" in my journal. I also noticed they all had an accountant, so I jotted that down, too. Based on Gary's questions, I knew I needed someone with marketing experience as well as someone who knew sales—like a real estate agent or a loan officer.

To fill these positions, I looked to people I knew personally who were up-and-coming in their career. I also thought about people I knew who already sat on a board and might be willing to give mine a try. Finally, I tried to go for diversity in terms of age, gender, and experience.

I suggest starting with five board members and then adding a few as you grow. I would not go above fifteen, even when you grow to be a multimillion-dollar organization. When too many people are involved, decision-making can become difficult, which wastes valuable time.

I also suggest having an odd number of board members so there's always a majority when voting. I found this out the hard way. When I first formed the board of directors, I only had four members; I was missing a marketing person. When we voted on a decision to spend a good amount of money, we ended up in a tie. It took us a few extra weeks of conversation to make a decision that could have been resolved in a matter of minutes if we had an odd number of people from the start.

For each of the positions on the board, I made a list of potential people, then I invited each one to meet me for coffee. At first, I thought I would take them to lunch or dinner, but then I realized I would be paying for the food and drinks at these meetings, and I didn't have any money. So, my first boardroom was a Starbucks because coffee is a lot cheaper than a meal.

In addition, lunch or dinner meetings have unpredictable aspects that can possibly hinder your pitch. It's hard to ask someone to help you when the server asks to refill your drink every time you try to speak. These interruptions can throw you off your game and then you have to start all over. Additionally, it can be challenging to focus if either of you have salad stuck in your teeth. You'll probably be nervous enough as it is, anticipating the other person's reaction and wondering if they will say yes; you don't need the extra distractions.

WHO SHOULDN'T SIT ON YOUR BOARD

I'm just going to say it: family members should not sit on your board. I get a lot of pushback on this one, so hear me out. I've read studies showing many mistakes for starting a board of directors. and having family members on a board of directors opens the door to problems.[1] Some of the biggest nonprofit scandals involve family members embezzling money and misusing funds. The board will vote on things like your salary, and having a family member vote yes to a substantial raise is a little fishy. It opens you up to liability, even when things are on the up and up. Also, I believe in total transparency. If I make a bad decision, I need my board to tell me. I don't want

---

1   Charity Lawyer, "Top 15 Nonprofit Board Governance Mistakes," *Board Charity Blog*, October 5, 2009, https://charitylawyerblog.com/2009/10/05/top-15-non-profit-board-governance-mistakes-from-a-legal-perspective/.

my dad to sweep it under the rug and act like it never happened because I'm his son.

Having family members on your board also opens the door to divisions within the family if you happen to hold opposing views. When you disagree in the boardroom you sure as heck don't want to take that disagreement home with you. The statement "Never mix family and business" rings true for nonprofits as well.

BOARD RESPONSIBILITIES AND LOGISTICS

The board of directors guides and governs the organization. They help with strategic planning as well as making hard and often unpopular decisions about finance, marketing, program growth, legal matters, by-laws, and sustainability.

The National Council of Nonprofits says the board of directors has three main duties:[2]

1. **Duty of Care:** Take care of the nonprofit by ensuring prudent use of all assets, including facility, people, and goodwill.
2. **Duty of Loyalty:** Ensure that the nonprofit's activities

---

2   National Council of Nonprofits, "Board Roles and Responsibilities," *Council of Nonprofits*, n.d., https://www.councilofnonprofits.org/tools-resources/board-roles-and-responsibilities.

and transactions are, first and foremost, advancing its mission; recognize and disclose conflicts of interest; make decisions that are in the best interest of the nonprofit corporation, not in the best interest of the individual board member (or any other individual or for-profit entity).

3. **Duty of Obedience:** Ensure that the nonprofit obeys applicable laws and regulations and follows its own bylaws, and that the nonprofit adheres to its stated corporate purposes/mission.

Over the years, these buckets have guided our board's decision-making and have helped us create many key policies.

In addition to governing, the board provides counsel to you, the mission driver, when you feel like throwing in the towel. It's nearly impossible to carry the load of your mission alone. By coaching me through some unexpected curveballs and misfortunes of business, my board has helped me stay in the game, and I am forever grateful for each of them. Make sure you have people who support not only the mission but also you.

At first, your board of directors will typically serve as your volunteer staff or leadership team, as they will probably help you do whatever needs to be done, in addition to making the big decisions. As you grow and have processes in place, however, it's important to form a new group to help you run the organization day to day so the board can focus on governing.

I formed what I called a test-hard, pivot-often leadership team about two years after Roc Solid began. The board of directors was creating various processes, and for the most part, I was the one implementing them. They were working, but I needed help to keep the momentum growing. Things change very quickly in the beginning, and you need a group of people who will jump in and help you with the day-to-day tasks.

The goal is to get the board of directors out of the day-to-day operations as soon as possible, so they can focus on the larger picture of growing the organization by opening doors that could lead to more donations to further the mission. Another plus to having the board out of the day-to-day is that when unique challenges arise, you have a fresh set of eyes to look at the issue at hand and give you a different perspective.

Boards usually meet once a month, and I recommend meeting on the same day of the week as opposed to the same date—for example, the second Tuesday of every month rather than the fifteenth or the thirtieth. This makes it easier for everyone to remember and helps with scheduling. I recommend sending out calendar invites once a year for all the meetings.

Make these meetings a priority. In the early stages, you will be exhausted and have the urge to cancel the meetings. Push through that. These meetings are extremely important, and showing up every month sets the tone for success in the future. For us, board members are allowed to miss two meetings per year. After the second time, one of the agenda items at the next meeting is to discuss that member's commitment to the board and the organization.

I guarantee that you will not agree with everything the board decides, but you cannot make them the bad guys. I did this in the beginning, and as a result, my staff and volunteers had a negative impression of the board. I lost a valuable board member because I was struggling with founder's syndrome and I let my pride get in the way (more on the pitfalls of founder's syndrome in Chapter 8). I made him out to be the bad boss, while I played the role of a good one. It's one of my biggest regrets to this day. I should have stepped up to the plate and taken the blame. Creating an us-versus-them mentality with the board is one of the biggest challenges I see in organizations I've consulted with.

To address this, I started changing my terminology.

When the board handed down unpopular decisions, I stopped saying, "The board decided this" and started saying, "*We* decided this." "*We*" represents the entire organization. When I walk out of the boardroom and use the word *we*, the organization moves forward because "we" stay united and focused. You are a team, and your staff and volunteers need to see it and hear it.

TERM LIMITS

When I researched the boards of directors for other nonprofits, I found that many of them did not have term limits. From my perspective, having the same people on the board for an indefinite amount of time leads to stagnation. So, from the beginning, our board members had three-year term limits, with a maximum of three terms. At the end of each three-year cycle, members have to be voted in to remain on the board. Looking back, creating term limits was one of the best things we did. It has kept ideas fresh, provided new perspectives, and helped us produce a new stream of donations when new members with new contacts come on to the board.

Having term limits can also help you let go of board members who are not pulling their weight, without having to fire them. It's hard to fire someone who is working for free. If you have a board member who isn't filling their commitments, consider how much time they have on their term and gear your conversation accordingly. I'm not saying that you should avoid confrontation and settle for dead weight, but you might be able to let the term limit do the hard work for you.

DIVISION OF POWER

As the founder and CEO, I figured I would also be the chairman of the board, but that was not the case. I quickly learned that power should be divided. Total autonomy in a nonprofit opens the door to many gray areas. There needs to be a system of checks and balances. As the CEO and mission driver, you will be going to the board for money. If you're also the chairman of the board, you have lost the ability to have someone else check your decision-making. It also puts a heavy burden on you when faced with major financial decisions.

In addition, leading an organization is hard, and you need a chairman and partner who can go into battle with you and share the burden. When you're feeling low, that person can lead the charge, and other times you will be the ones on the front line. To this day, I have never been chairman of the board. Having someone else in charge of the board means that if I am not doing my job, I could get fired from the organization that I created. Having this accountability and split in authority and power has made me strive to become a better leader and CEO. It has helped me stay accountable and has pushed me out of my comfort zone many times.

AGENDAS AND MORE

After I found a lawyer, accountant, marketing guru, and sales expert, I rallied everyone together for our first board meeting. Everyone showed up on time—except me. I strolled in about fifteen minutes late, greeted everyone, then took a seat. "So, what are we going to talk about?" I asked half-wittedly.

At that point, my brilliant-but-tough-as-nails finance guy, Jerry, asked with flames in his eyes, "Hey, can I talk to you for a minute?" He was not smiling.

We stepped aside, and Jerry ripped into me. "If you want me to be a part of this dream of yours, you will never be late again. Matter of fact, you're going to be fifteen minutes early. *And* you're going to have a written agenda for every single meeting because our time is important, *and* you just disrespected everybody here because you came late, *and* you weren't ready for this meeting. Are you serious about this? Because if you're not, I'm done. I'm not going to waste any more of my time."

That was the punch in the gut that I needed. For the last twelve years, I have been fifteen minutes early to every single board meeting, with a prepared agenda. To show my appreciation of the members' time I also provide bottled water and snacks for each member.

When I created my first agenda, I needed help. I had no idea what to put on an agenda or where to even start. I jumped online, did a little research, and discovered *Robert's Rules of Order* (robertsrules.com). I learned that an agenda includes a call to order, a chairman's report, and a vice chairperson's report, approval of minutes, secretary and treasurer's report (note to self: that means I also need a chairperson and a vice chairperson...). With a little more research, I learned about the different roles:

- Chairperson: oversees the board of directors, leads the meetings, provides counsel to you as the mission driver, speaks at events on your behalf
- Vice chairperson: leads meetings if the chairman is not present, recruits new board members, makes sure you are hitting your goals as an organization
- Treasurer: reports on the money and the financial health of the organization
- Secretary: keeps minutes of the board meetings, updates the bylaws, sends meeting reminders, and responsible for getting people to the meetings

Often your finance person will be the treasurer, but not

always. In my case, my finance guy was my first treasurer and my first chairperson. Because Jerry was highly skilled in budget management and was the only board member with board experience, he was the best choice for both positions.

We vote on these four roles once a year. One major reason we vote yearly is that we do not want anyone to feel like they have a free ride. You have to work hard to be on our board, and we want people to take it seriously. Just because someone is the vice chairperson doesn't mean they will be the chairperson, especially if they did not perform well as vice chair. We vote yearly, because that's what we established in our bylaws, but you may decide to handle it differently (more on bylaws shortly).

LEGAL ASPECTS

After forming my board of directors, I turned to the legal issues: incorporation, the organizational bylaws, and the 501(c)(3) classification. For each of these areas, I relied heavily on the expertise of the attorney who had joined my board of directors.

Your lawyer is there to keep you safe today, tomorrow, and ten years from now. In the very beginning, my attorney warned me about things I never thought would happen. I figured we were doing something nice for people; why would anyone sue us or try to take us to court? When you're focused on the mission, it's easy to overlook situations that could have negative legal ramifications for you and your organization. The day of Jillian's build, it never crossed my mind to have everyone—both volunteers and Jillian's parents—sign waivers stating they wouldn't sue us. I was focused on doing good, on changing the life of that little girl. Thankfully, nothing happened that day, except for building hope.

Even if you don't want to think about things like liability and lawsuits when it comes to charity work, doing so will serve your organization and your mission because it ensures you will be able to continue helping others. Get a lawyer to help you think ahead about such things.

BYLAWS

My research told me that one of the things boards of directors do is manage and upkeep the bylaws. This, of course, caused me to wonder, *What the heck are bylaws?* As I learned, bylaws are the rules that govern an organization. They also outline the term limits of the board of directors, how many members will sit on the board, and what their positions will be. When you file the paperwork for your 501(c)(3) (to be discussed shortly), you have to submit bylaws and proof of incorporation as part of the process.

I had no idea what laws should govern an organization, so I found a sample set of bylaws I could download and print. I highlighted everything I agreed with and then typed them into a new document (I'm a touch-it, feel-it kind of guy; you could simply cut and paste instead of printing a hard copy). I inserted the Roc Solid Foundation name at the top and gave them to my attorney to make them legal. You can find a sample set of bylaws at my website, thenewmanexperience.com.

Bylaws aren't something that you write, put in a drawer, and never look at again. As your organization grows and changes, your bylaws will need to grow and change as well. I recommend reviewing your bylaws once a year to make sure they are still accurate. Did you add a couple of board members, but your bylaws state you will have no more than five? Did you change the time of your monthly board meetings? It's easy to overlook relatively small changes like this, which is why the board and I review our bylaws every October and then vote on them in December to be ready for the next year. The attorney on your board can help you make sure the updates are all done correctly.

INCORPORATION AND 501(C)(3)

The first step to becoming an official nonprofit is to incorporate at the state level. This involves filing Articles of Incorporation and makes you a legal corporate entity, or business. Organizing as a corporation also provides liability protection for the board of directors and key operators in the organization.

After you incorporate, the next step is to file for 501(c) (3) status from the IRS. A 501(c)(3) classification allows an organization to become a charity. Approval on the standard filing takes anywhere between two and twelve months. We snail-mailed our application and got approved in three months, but now you can submit it online. Prior to doing so, I suggest that you spend a little money and have an attorney review it for you.

When you file for your 501(c)(3), the IRS will ask you to include your bylaws to help them understand what you are trying to accomplish through your nonprofit. They also ask for a clear mission statement on why you exist. At the time we filed for our 501(c)(3), our mission statement was "to build hope for children with pediatric cancer and their families during the worst time of their life." We chose not to include our specific playset solution so we would have flexibility to change as we evolved as an organization. We will always build hope for children fighting cancer, but we may find additional or different models for doing this in the future (more on marrying your mission not your model in Chapter 7).

HOW TO WRITE A MISSION STATEMENT

A mission statement explains why you exist as an organization. It identifies what you do and who you do it for. As I said, the IRS will ask for this mission statement when you file for 501(c)(3) status, but that's not the only reason to write one. A mission statement also creates focus and direction for your nonprofit. It provides a framework that helps you stay in your lane and not creep into programs that take you away from your main purpose (more on mission creep in Chapter 7).

Here's a basic formula to help you knock out a first draft of your mission statement:

_____ [organization name] will _____ [what you do] for _____ [target audience]

For us, that would look like this:

Roc Solid Foundation will build hope for every child fighting cancer.

After you have the basics, start developing your ideas. Try to use high-impact words that communicate exactly what you're hoping to accomplish. I also recommend keeping it short and sweet, preferably one sentence but no more than three.

As your organization grows and gains momentum, revisit your mission statement to make sure that each word is necessary and is as impactful as possible. For example, our original mission statement was:

To build hope for children with pediatric cancer and their families during the worst time of their life

Over time we evaluated each word and eliminated several that weren't needed. We also realized that there's no hope in the word "with" so we changed it to "fighting." The word "fighting" implies that kids are owning cancer and pushing back. Our current mission statement is much shorter and more direct:

To build hope for kids fighting cancer

I suggest that you brainstorm until you have three working versions. Then spend some time with your core group to evaluate the options and create a final statement. One way to do this is to write all three versions on a whiteboard using a different color for each statement. Then circle the most powerful words in each statement and drop them to a fourth version. Polish and wordsmith this one until you and your group are satisfied.

Don't be afraid to get feedback! Once you have a polished statement, say it to your family and friends to see what they like and don't like and what they remember. Ultimately, that's the bottom line: you want people to remember who you are, what you're doing, and who you're doing it for. The shorter and more precise your statement is, the more likely people are to remember it.

When I filed my 501(c)(3), I asked three or four accountants to help me file the paperwork, and they all refused. They all said starting a nonprofit during the worst economy since the Great Depression was a horrible idea.

Then I remembered seeing on social media that one of my buddies had graduated from law school. We hadn't seen or spoken to each other in a couple of years, but I figured I had nothing to lose. I invited him to join me for a couple of beers, and I laid out all my hopes and dreams. To lighten his decision-making, I made sure that he had a few beers before I asked, "So would you be willing to help me file a 501(c)(3)?" Then I held my breath.

He looked right back at me and said, "Sure, why not."

I was so caught off guard that I ended up spitting out half of my beer. I regained my composure and asked, "What did you say?"

"Sure, why not. What do we have to lose?"

Not only did he agree to help us with the filing of the 501(c)(3), he also agreed to help with all the legal aspects of starting the organization and joined my original board of directors. The lesson here? The answer is always no if you don't ask.

FINANCES

When I began filing the paperwork to incorporate and register our 501(c)(3), I quickly realized I needed money to pay for these things and run my charity. I also realized this money would be coming from donations. People would be giving me money and trusting me to do good with it. I felt the weight of that responsibility and decided that Roc Solid Foundation would have no gray areas. We would make sure every penny in and out was accounted for.

If you don't keep your financial house in order, you could lose big potential donors, as well as credibility. Once you lose the credibility related to managing other people's hard-earned money, it is almost impossible to get it back. People make sure a professional, organized money management system is in place before they are comfortable donating to nonprofits. Without those donations, you won't have the money to build the organization you're trying to build. At the end of the day, the money is not yours or the board of directors'. You are only stewards who are responsible to use the money for the purpose it was given: to further your mission.

In construction, I was an excellent tradesman and a horrible businessman. My company failed because of my financial model, or lack thereof. When I started Roc Solid Foundation, I kept receipts in a shoebox in my closet. That was the extent of my financial system.

Clearly, I needed help, so I decided to educate myself. I found that there were two important aspects I needed to have a handle on: budgets and financial statements. This is where the CPA or accountant comes into play on the board of directors.

DIRECTORS AND OFFICERS INSURANCE

The number-one question potential board members ask is whether we have directors and officers insurance. Whereas general liability covers the organization as a whole, directors and officers insurance covers board members' personal assets if something were to happen during a program event or fundraiser. If a child fell off the swing on the playset we built, for example, every board member could be sued. Directors and officers insurance protects them up to the amount you choose.

In addition, directors and officers insurance pays for lawsuits related to the decisions made by the board of directors, and they make a lot of major decisions about how your nonprofit is run. They establish an organization's goals and strategies, determine how funds are spent, and set salaries for employees. They need liability protection for their decisions.

BUDGET

The budget allows you to think about the entire organization and estimate the money going out and coming in each year. In the beginning you'll be guessing at the amounts for each category in your budget, but that's okay. You'll soon get a good idea of what you spend each year.

When I created our first budget, I started with expenses because they're easier to identify and project. Think about everything you might possibly spend in a year to successfully run your organization with no gray areas. Here's a short list to get you started:

- Car maintenance (fuel, repairs, insurance)
- Cell phone
- Computer
- Development (fundraising expenses, venues, DJs, decorations)
- Directors and officers insurance
- Food (to feed volunteers, pay for dinner with potential donors)
- Internet
- Liability insurance
- Marketing and social media (brochures, business cards, ads, website)
- Program cost (expenses to accomplish your mission)
- Rent/lease
- T-shirts
- Utilities

At first you might have a miscellaneous bucket to cover things you hadn't thought of ahead of time, but as your organization grows and you learn what you spend money on, the items in that miscellaneous category should be given their line in the budget. When you analyze the financials with your accountant at the end of *each month*, look at what you actually spent money on and add that to your budget. Don't wait until the end of the year to get your books in order. Trust me, you will save yourself a bunch of headaches and unnecessary stress if you keep the house (your books) in order all year long.

FINANCIAL STATEMENTS

When I was starting, my accountant emphasized one thing over and over: it's not your money. Whether someone gives you $5 or $500,000, the gift is a huge deal, because people are choosing to give to you and your organization. They are trusting you. It is your core responsibility to properly document all money received into and spent by the organization.

In the simplest terms, financial statements are "written records that convey the business activities and financial performance of a company." The most common financial statements are the income or profit and loss statement, the balance sheet, and the statement of cash flows. Your finance guy can help you with the particulars on all three of these. At this point it's important to know that you need official written documents to account for money in and out, not receipts in a shoebox or purchases written on a napkin. These documents are often audited by the IRS, and big donors will likely ask to see them as well.

In a nonprofit, the board of directors is responsible for approving the financial statement on a regular basis. Every month, our board votes on the Roc Solid financial statement to make sure our nonprofit is in good standing—that every single penny in and out is counted and accounted for.

How can the board vote on receipts stuffed into a shoe-box? They can't. We needed a better system, so we quickly moved to QuickBooks. My accountant helped me create a chart of accounts, so that every expense could be classified. For example, we have accounts for programs, fundraising, food, and much more. My accountant also helped me create a budget to guide how much we spent in each area.

We're all busy. It's easy to lose track of receipts in the midst of daily activities. You might buy something for an event and then take your daughter to practice and then go home to cook dinner, and two days later realize you don't know where the receipt is for the item you purchased. Not having a receipt is a gray area. Don't let this happen. There are so many ways to keep track of receipts electronically. For example, whenever I spend money, I immediately take a picture of the receipt with my phone and add it to the monthly expense folder on Google Drive. It's easy. No gray areas.

You would be surprised how often I get asked for my most recent approved financial statement. When someone is asking me for the approved statements, they are typically looking to see if we have a financial system in place to manage the money they are considering donating to our organization. They are making sure that more than one person has their eye on the finances of the organization. If you are asked for a financial statement and you can't provide one, that donor will probably give their money to someone who is more prepared.

SUSTAINABILITY

Gary also asked about my sustainability model. As I later found out, he was asking what we were doing to create a sustainable revenue source to fuel my mission. A one-time or even once-a-year donation of $10,000 is not sustainable. A sustainability model involves development and fundraising to generate consistent income.

As the organization grew, I found myself yet again sitting in front of a man who was known in the community for his philanthropy. Judge Bray, or "the Judge," as everyone called him, was one of the most well-respected men I've ever met. His foundation issues grants to nonprofits.

As I sat in his office, navigating the conversation that involved me asking for $10,000, the Judge said in his soft-spoken tone, "Eric, I have been doing this for many years now, and I have gifted a lot of amazing organizations over the years. A problem that I see in nonprofits is that there is no sustainability model. If I give you this $10,000 this year, nine times out of ten, people will come back next year asking for more. Mr. Newman, I will not be able to grant you the money this year. Come back when you have a sustainable model."

At that point, I was used to hearing the word *no* from other foundations and companies. This time was different. He gave me something to research and look into. I was intrigued to find out how I could be different.

I spent the next year looking at how we could make our organization sustainable by creating multiple revenue streams. For one of these streams, I came up with a plan for selling playset builds as a corporate team-building exercise. When I went back to the Judge, I presented this idea and asked, "Is this a sustainable model?"

"Brilliant," he said and awarded me the $10,000 grant. We ended up purchasing a box truck with the money, and that truck is still building playsets for kids fighting cancer today.

NOT EASY BUT WORTH IT

Over the last twelve years, I've shared Gary's list of questions with many people who are trying to start a nonprofit to turn their pain into their purpose. In each case, the last item on that list is a task to come find me when they check off all the rest. Less than 10 percent actually do.

Most people quit in the process of laying the foundation for their nonprofit because it's tedious, it's boring, and it's definitely not sexy. Building a solid, sustainable non-profit is not always easy, but it's always worth it.

Don't skip this step just because it's hard. If you do, the house—your organization—will fall. At the same time, don't quit just because it's hard. Find the people who are smarter than you and ask for help. People love to give advice, but we often don't ask. Just ask. And for God's sake, google it.

After you lay the foundation, it's time to tell people what you're doing and develop the program to get it done. The next chapter can help you start.

Chapter 3

DESIGN THE PROGRAM

When we started gaining momentum with Roc Solid Foundation, we had an opportunity to take our mission on the road one hundred miles away. We could only afford one hotel room, so all seven or eight of us packed into one room.

After the build, I took the crew out for pizza and beer and then headed back to the hotel with one of my buddies. I was wearing a brand-new "I Am Roc Solid" T-shirt, and when an older couple joined us in the elevator, the man looked at my shirt and asked, "Hey, what is Roc Solid?"

I gave him my name and title and then launched into my entire journey, but by the time the couple's floor approached, I hadn't even told them our actual mission. The elevator stopped and the couple was gone.

My buddy looked at me and said, "You lost that one, boss." That couple could have been my first million-dollar donors, and I lost them because I didn't know how to briefly explain my nonprofit's mission.

When I started Roc Solid Foundation, I followed the plan I've presented so far: I narrowed down the problem and solution, created an action list, decided on a name, and then built the unsexy foundation. Then I dove into developing a program to deliver the solution without figuring out how to clearly and concisely tell people what I was doing. As my elevator experience shows, that's not the best way to go about it.

So, we'll start this chapter by discussing how to create a simple but powerful elevator pitch, and then talk about how to plan your program and start putting your vision into practice.

FORMULATE YOUR ELEVATOR PITCH

An elevator pitch is just like it sounds: a statement you can deliver in the time it takes to ride an elevator with someone. That means you need to be able to share the important information in less than a minute. Your pitch should be short, easy to say, and memorable.

Some people spend lots of time trying to come up with

a creative pitch, but it's better to be clear than clever. If you can't be clear in a minute or less, you're going to lose your audience, so it won't matter how clever you are.

The pitch should briefly state the who, what, why, and how of your idea. For example, here's mine:

I build playsets for kids fighting cancer. I had cancer when I was three, and I lost two cousins to this horrible disease. Then, in my twenties, I owned a construction company. In 2008, I lost everything, so I combined my passions for construction and pediatric cancer and started a nonprofit.

After you write your elevator pitch, you have to practice it. The more you say it, the more polished it will become and the more naturally you will be able to share it. Don't just practice in the mirror. Deliver your pitch to others and be willing to receive feedback. Don't get bent out of shape if someone starts fake yawning or suggests changing a few words. If your buddy is bored, how are you going to hook someone who has no obligation to talk to you in the first place? The only way to polish something is by creating friction, and feedback provides that friction. Polishing will rub out the rough spots and help you create an elevator pitch people will remember.

Your pitch should hold the other person's attention long

enough for you to follow up with a power statement—a short, unforgettable statement designed to grab the person's attention so that they ask questions in the moment and keep thinking about your organization after the conversation ends. Ultimately, you want these questions to lead to collecting contact information for a potential volunteer and/or donor.

When you create a power statement, follow the original Twitter principle: express your point in 140 characters or less. If you can't say it in a tweet, it's not short or simple enough. Keep massaging your power statement until it's something a six-year-old could understand. As Albert Einstein once said, "If you can't explain it to a six-year-old, you don't understand it yourself."

As with your pitch, coming up with an effective power statement will take some work. In the beginning of Roc Solid, I told my buddy, "Man, these playsets kill cancer!"

"Well, they don't kill cancer," he said.

"Okay, you're right. But they allow kids to play. Kids fighting cancer may ultimately lose the war, but they can still win a battle. Those playsets allow them to escape the reality of cancer, even for a little bit."

That conversation led me to wordsmith and polish my

idea until I came up with this power statement: "Play defeats cancer."

To work on your power statement, I recommend going back to your journal. Yup, you guessed it—do another brain dump around the pain point and the solution. Then use a thesaurus and search for significant, powerful words that will catch people's attention. Ask for feedback until you land on something that fits.

As your organization grows and you figure out exactly what you're doing, you'll likely develop more than one power statement. Remember, the goal is to get the person to ask questions, so you might use a different power statement with different people, depending on the direction of the conversation. Two of my other power statements are "We can't change the fact that kids have cancer, but we can change how they live with it" and "I guarantee we will show you what hope looks like."

You should be able to complete the whole elevator pitch and power statement, and collect their information, in three minutes or less. People are busy. Respect their time and be prepared to deliver a focused message.

Here's an example of how a conversation might happen where an elevator pitch and power statement come into play:

I settle into my seat on a plane and nod to the guy sitting next to me. As we're both pulling our earbuds out of our bags, he asks, "What brought you to LA?"

"I build playsets for kids fighting cancer," I say.

The person pauses. "You do what?"

"I build playsets for kids fighting cancer. We travel the US building the sets in their backyards so they can just be a kid."

"What got you into this line of work?"

"I had cancer when I was three. Then, in my twenties, I owned a construction company, but in 2008, I lost everything, so I combined my passions for construction and pediatric cancer and started this nonprofit."

"Wow. How long have you been doing that?"

"Twelve years now. The organization is called Roc Solid Foundation, and we build playsets because we believe play defeats cancer."

"Woah. That's a bold statement. What do you mean?"

The whole goal of the elevator pitch and power statement is

to get the person to questions that involve "tell me more." If you don't get there, you lose the deal. The person will be putting in his earbuds before you can share your mission and how he can be involved. In the beginning, I was famous for drawing out the conversation by adding a bunch of unnecessary words to sound fancier than I was. It didn't work. Take away the fluff and allow your mission to speak for itself. Be precise with your words. They have extreme power and meaning when they come from a place of purpose.

You never know who you're going to be riding an elevator with or sitting next to on a plane. Be ready! It could be your first million-dollar donor.

It's crucial to hone your elevator pitch and power statement because you can't do the next part—build your program, put it into action, and fund it—by yourself. You need people to give of their time, talent, and treasures, but they can't do that if they don't know what you're doing. This idea may have been bouncing around in your brain for years, but now you have to explain it in a clear and concise way so that others can understand what you're doing and, more importantly, wrap their hearts around it. When you change people's hearts, you change the direction of their lives and actions will follow. Our hearts rarely forget things that leave an impact. To move people to join your mission, you have to touch their hearts, and that starts with a simple, brief elevator pitch.

> If you change the heart, you
> change the direction of a life.

DEVELOP, TEST, PIVOT

Starting a nonprofit is a unique chance to create your own vision. The opportunities are endless and the sky's the limit.

Still, it's easy to get caught up in the comparison game. I know I did early on. While you don't want to reinvent the wheel, you also don't want to do something just because everyone else is doing it.

One of the biggest tragedies I have seen in the nonprofit world is when an organization becomes a cover band, playing someone else's music. Don't get me wrong; I love a good cover band. But cover bands do not change the world. This is your opportunity to write your own lyrics about your experiences, to figure out how you can uniquely help someone go through the same problem you did.

No matter what your pain point or who you're helping, the program is the heart of your organization. It's everything between the problem and the solution. It's how you're going to solve the pain point, who's going to help, how it will happen, how you will pay for it, when and where it will happen, and more.

Jason is one of the guys I've walked through the process of starting a nonprofit. In his younger years, Jason had some experiences that left him stuck and in need of help. His nonprofit focuses on solving this problem for men experiencing homelessness. He meets these men right where they are and invites them to participate in a program that provides interview training and other life skills to help them get off the streets. Getting suits for the men to wear to an interview, creating the resumé-writing program, finding volunteers—that's all part of the program Jason developed to deliver his solution.

I am also helping Darlene and Ryan through this process. Their daughter Kaylee fought a neuroblastoma for nine years. As her cancer progressed, Kaylee was stuck in the hospital for weeks at a time, and one of her favorite activities was building Legos. As Kaylee lost motor skills in her hands, her dad would hold the instruction book, Kaylee would pick up the piece and hand it to her dad, and he would put it in the right spot. This time together created memories for her dad to hold onto, and the family still has Lego creations that Kaylee created with her own hands. The problem Darlene and Ryan found is that the hospital didn't have Legos; the family had to bring their own for Kaylee to build. Their solution is to stock Legos at the hospital so children who are stuck in their beds can build with their family and create amazing memories. Their program is still being developed, but the goal is to get Lego sets into hospitals in their home state.

For me, the problem lies with children like my cousin Nicole, who didn't have a safe place to play because cancer and treatment gave her a compromised immune system. Our solution is providing that safe, clean place: a playset in their own backyard. Everything in between—designing the playset, buying materials, finding volunteers, organizing the builds, teaching people how to build the sets—is all part of the program.

ASK WHAT'S MISSING

Go back to your list of nonprofits that are solving a similar problem. Was there anything missing in the way they were going about it? Could you create a program to fill that gap? This step can be challenging. It's easy to see what reality currently is. In developing the program, you need to see things as they can be.

As I was thinking through the gaps that could be filled, I found myself searching online for images related to the problem I was trying to solve. I printed them out and posted them on my walls.

Then I drew circles around the pain points in each photo: the little boy in a hospital bed, the bald little girl looking sad. The circles gave me a target, something to aim at. Then I started thinking about how I could hit those bullseyes. How could I bring my playset solution into reality?

Whether you print out photos, create a file on your Google Drive, or create a mind map in your journal, give yourself a target. Then start figuring out how to hit it. This is where things get practical. The program you create will take you from problem to solution and make up the day-to-day nuts and bolts of your organization.

LIST YOUR SKILLS

As you consider how to deliver your solution, ask yourself, "What am I good at? What skills and knowledge do I bring to the table?" Make a list in your journal. Also spend some time thinking about what you absolutely cannot stand to do, and write those things down as well. Then consider how both lists correlate to the problem you're trying to solve. Don't design a program around something you don't like to do or skills you don't have. This process is hard enough; going outside your skill set will only increase your frustration.

I'm good at building things. I can see the finished product before I even start. Building playsets was a natural fit since it uses my construction talent to provide play and solve the problem.

Jason, the guy who has started a nonprofit to help men get off the streets, knows how to engage anyone in easy, comfortable conversation. He is able to look past differences and talk to people right where they are, without judgment. This is a natural fit with talking to men experiencing homelessness and inviting them to be part of a program that empowers them by providing suits and interview training.

I also spent some time coaching Stephanie through this process of turning her pain into her purpose. Stephanie and her husband had previously gone through some financial challenges, and as a result, their credit took a nosedive. Through her business, Stephanie offers credit repair solutions to get them ready to make major purchases such as homes, and other major investments they may need good credit for.

In terms of skills, Stephanie has no problem with confrontation, and she refuses to take no for an answer. She uses both of these talents when she calls credit card companies to help clients get their credit repaired so they can buy a home.

To use your skills to the fullest, you might consider taking a strengths finder survey. Though there are a bunch of personality tests out there, my two favorites are DISC and Enneagram because the results are the most accurate and easiest to remember and implement. There are free versions of both available on the internet, and if you like what you learn, you can pay for a more in-depth study. Trust me, this will be money well spent. One hint: when you're taking the test, make sure you don't overthink the questions. Your initial response is usually the right one.

KEEP IT SIMPLE

When my dad and I built a playset for my buddy Keith's daughter, it took us more than twenty agonizing hours. I knew I needed to simplify that process if I wanted to get volunteers involved in building playsets through Roc Solid. My golden rule now is to respect simplicity—I try to make things as simple as possible, simple enough that a sixth grader could understand it.

You may have the idea for your nonprofit. It may be based on the pain you experienced and the solution you wish you had. But alone, you cannot bring that solution to the community you're trying to serve. You will need the help of many volunteers, and the best way to get them involved is to make it easy for them to do so. Good intentions don't change the world. You need to deliberately design a simple program so people can help you execute it and move your mission forward.

By keeping it simple, you make it easy for people to see,

touch, and feel what you're doing. Focus on creating that feel-it moment in your program, the moment when someone's life is changed and the problem is solved— the moment when little Jillian comes running around the corner, for example. When someone can see the problem being solved, when they can actually get their hands on the solution, they'll wrap their heart around what you're doing and join in your mission. (See Chapter 5 for more on recruiting, engaging, and retaining volunteers.)

TEST YOUR IDEA

I committed to our first build before I had the program in place. I didn't know how long it would take, who would help me build it, how I would feed the volunteers, or how I would pay for it all. I had to test my idea without having all the answers.

When people build airplanes, they do it when the plane is on the ground, not flying through the sky. Testing your program, however, is probably going to feel like building an airplane at thirty thousand feet, going full speed. I promise you that oxygen is still flowing even when you feel like you can't breathe.

This testing phase is hard. I can almost guarantee it won't go perfectly the first time. However, if you were able to go through the pain you've already experienced, there's nothing you can't do.

Once the first test project is complete, I recommend that you reconvene with the same people who were instrumental in helping you with the project. Try to meet with them twenty-four to forty-eight hours after the test run, while the project is still fresh in their minds. Discussing what went right, what was a disaster, and how to improve the next time is vital for future success. You might also ask:

- How far off budget were we? Did we even have a budget?
- How many people showed up? Could we have used more volunteers? How many?
- Did we have enough food to feed the volunteers?

During this meeting, be careful not to talk the entire time. Allow other people to get their opinions out first and then add yours. Because of your extreme passion toward this program, you will tend to have the loudest voice, but some of the best ideas come from the softest whisper, and that whisper usually comes from someone else.

Another part of testing your program is telling family and friends what's been laid on your heart. Fair warning: some people won't think this is a good idea, either because they don't understand what you're trying to accomplish, or they are worried about you opening up old wounds. Don't let that stop you. Even if the first test drive has lots of problems, you're still moving the ball forward. You're figuring out what works and what doesn't.

Before the first build for Jillian, I met with some very influential men in my life. I told them the plan and asked for their support. The response was not positive. Toward the end of the meeting, I reminded them what my dad had always told me as a child—that if I could beat cancer, I could do anything—and then I left.

For a couple weeks, I wrestled with their feedback and what to do. We didn't have the money to build this playset. I still didn't have the people power lined up. But I knew that Jillian was counting on me. I decided to move forward anyway.

When I decided to sell Krispy Kremes to fund that first build, I went back to the same men and presented a clear plan for how I was going to accomplish the first project. I told them that I was going to focus on one project at a time and asked if they would support this first one. Because I took time to add a little more vision to my plan, they decided to help with the project, and they sold the most Krispy Kremes by far.

That encounter with the "haters," if you will, led me to a simple idea that I carried forward in my planning: focus on one project, one child at a time. Do for that one little girl or boy what I ultimately want to do for the many. The grand vision burning in your soul might be too grand for others to understand. That's okay. Use the haters to fuel your passion and fine-tune your program.

Designing your program and getting it off the ground isn't going to be easy, but you can't let the problems of today dictate the decisions for tomorrow. Look at your 'why photo.' Think about how your solution will help people who are experiencing that specific pain point you suffered through once before.

You can't let the problems of today dictate the decisions for tomorrow.

After you've tested your idea and seen the fruit of your labor, it's time to sit down and think, both on your own and with your board of directors. It's time to establish values to guide your organization and the decisions you make as its leader.

Chapter 4

VALUES MATTER

In the early days of Roc Solid Foundation, my mom and I were in our world headquarters, also known as my parents' garage. "What's the one thing you remember from the day I was diagnosed with cancer?" I asked her.

She didn't answer me until about two weeks later when I was sitting at my desk. "You know what I remember about that day?" my mom said out of the blue. "I remember that your dad had to leave me on the worst day of my life to go pack an overnight bag. Your dad is my rock, and I didn't know what to do when he left me at the hospital with you. I had never felt so alone."

I looked at her for a few seconds, trying to grasp the weight of her words. "Well, why don't we eradicate that moment from the face of the earth? No family should ever be split up on the day their child is diagnosed with cancer."

And just like that, Roc Solid Ready Bags were born. Almost immediately we started designing a program to get the bags into the hands of every family who hears the words "Your child has cancer." My mom and I devised a list of necessary items to go inside those bags: standard his and her toiletries, a roll of quarters for the vending machines, a blanket for the cold hospital rooms, a flashlight so parents can easily navigate the room without waking Baby Bear, a tablet with games for the child who is now confined to a hospital bed, and my favorite: a hair tie. It is one of the cheapest items in the bag and it may seem irrelevant, but to a Mama Bear who is spending hours hunched over a hospital bed, her hair falling into her face while she is trying to comfort her child, it is very significant. These Ready Bags have all the essentials to show parents that someone out there knows exactly what they're going through. These bags represent what hope looks like when the situation is not what you were hoping for at all.

I was and still am passionate about these Ready Bags. I know firsthand what they mean for a family who has just received the devastating news that their child has cancer.

About six months after we launched the Ready Bags, I met with a very large organization to request funding for the program. After I shared the details, the gentleman said, "We want to get involved. Give me a second," and walked out of the room.

The guy left the room and returned with an envelope, which he slid across the table. "Go ahead, you can open it."

Inside was a check for $10,000. Tears filled my eyes. As an organization, we've never seen such a large amount; it felt like we hit the nonprofit lotto.

"We truly believe in what you're doing," the businessman said. "We would love to be the first to rally behind your mission."

Filled with gratitude, I thanked him repeatedly and explained how this was going to be a game changer for the organization. This was the shot of momentum we had been waiting for. A business of this size believing in our small, relatively unknown startup nonprofit would instantly give us the street credit to keep loving and serving kids fighting cancer.

The businessman then disclosed that the check would come with a few stipulations. They wanted to include a branded bobblehead, Frisbee, and a few coupons for their services in each Roc Solid Ready Bag.

I understand it's a win-win world. You have to play the game. However, as the businessman talked, one of the Roc Solid values popped into my head: Families First. I had written down this statement time and time again. Families First. It was like a loud song running through my mind, beating inside my chest, over and over. *Families* First.

The last thing a family in this situation needs is to feel like they are being sold something, and that's exactly what those branded items would communicate.

We were not creating golf goody bags or birthday party favors. We were providing bags to bring hope and a glimmer of light in a dark situation. I had an MMA fight going on in my head. This guy was generously giving us money we really needed to stay afloat. That $10,000 would put a bag in the hands of many families who desperately needed it. But the stipulations didn't align with our values or the intentions of the bags.

I visualized a mom and dad holding that Frisbee: they are likely still in shock that their child has cancer, and now they have a brand new Frisbee to play with? It just didn't make sense, and I couldn't do it.

I slid that $10,000 check back across the table and said with tears in my eyes, "I'm sorry. This is not what's best for our families." And then I explained the mission of the bags again and how the stipulations weren't going to fit with our organization at this time.

In the nonprofit world, money blinds you faster than anything. I can't tell you how many times I have heard the statement "No money, no mission" because nonprofits rely on generous donations like this one to accomplish their mission. We could have paid for a lot of bags with that check; it could have been the break that we had been waiting for. Anything can be rationalized.

An interesting thing happened after I slid the check back and voiced my concerns. The businessman said, "Wait, we can renegotiate. I didn't mean to offend you." Maybe he heard the Families First tune in my head or caught a glimpse of my credibility because I stood by my values. A week later, we met again, and he gave us another check without the attached expectations. He trusted me with his money even more than he had before.

My board of directors and I had created the values for Roc Solid Foundation about six months before that business meeting. If we had not created a Families First value, if it had not been burned into my heart, I would have been blinded by the money. I truly believe that was a defining moment in both my career and my personal life, to stay true to that small voice and stand for what I believe. Having my value firmly in place enabled me to make that incredibly tough decision on the spot.

I still rely on those values every day. They help me with hiring new employees. They help me with financial decisions. They help me navigate hard conversations. They help me keep the main thing the main thing: to build hope for kids fighting cancer.

In this chapter we'll talk about why creating a few personal, unique values—not twenty-five that no one remembers—is so important. We'll also talk about how to create values and to help your volunteers and team members remember them and live them out.

WHY CREATE VALUES

In the *Pirates of the Caribbean* movies, Captain Jack Sparrow experienced chaos left and right, but through it all he had a unique compass guiding him to what he wanted most.

That's what values are: an inner compass that points to what is most important. Without this guidance, we can easily get lost at sea as we are knocked around by the challenges and setbacks that come along with starting a nonprofit or leading one.

In your excitement to begin helping people, you might be tempted to take a shortcut on values. Don't do it. The prep work here will lay the groundwork for your purpose to stand on for many years to come.

Values are the heart of the organization. Just as the heart

pumps life into the body, values pump life into your organization. If the heart stops pumping, the body dies; the same goes for your organization. When values are ingrained into your organization, your nonprofit will live out its purpose in every decision and action.

In case you need additional convincing, here are a few more reasons to create values:

Values help you make tough decisions. I would not have been able to say no to that $10,000 check without my value in place, and saying yes would not have been in the best interests of kids fighting cancer or their parents. This is perhaps the most important reason for creating values at the very beginning, right after you get your board of directors in place. They guide you to do the right things for the right reasons.

Values create credibility. If you create and live out your values from the beginning, you are likely to attract the attention of other like-minded people. Showing that you know what you stand for, that you walk the walk, gives you credibility. Values help you stand tall even when you are small.

Values point to what matters most. Values are the needle on the compass, pointing to the direction you should take in any given situation. The larger the ship, the farther away from shore it can travel and the easier it is to get lost, so the need for a compass is even greater. The same is true of an organization as it grows and more people start inserting their opinions. A compass is most useful when you lose sight of land, hit a few storms, and get turned around. It helps you stay the course when the journey gets rough and allows you to stay anchored to what matters most: the mission and the community you are called to love and serve.

I can't promise that it is going to be easy—in fact, it's likely going to be hard as hell—but I can promise you'll be able to lay your head down at night and know you made the right decisions based on what's most important to you and your organization.

Values help you stand tall even when you are small.

Values help you stand out. If your organization blends in, it will be forgotten. If you have a few core values that are personal and unique, you will stand out. In his book *Purple Cow: Transform Your Business by Being Remarkable,* Seth Godin emphasizes the importance of standing out in a crowded marketplace because if you don't, it's like you're invisible. I have driven past a few cow pastures. I have seen white cows, black cows, and spotted cows, but I have never seen a purple cow. If I ever do see a purple cow in a field of normal-looking cows, I will stop, take a photo, and never forget that moment. A purple cow stands out. Creating unique values for your organization helps you be the purple cow in the mass pasture of other organizations.

Values create culture. I have heard it said many times that culture isn't just something; it's everything. According to one definition, culture is a way of life. It's the beliefs, values, attitudes, morals, and behaviors that characterize a certain group of people, whether it's a society or an organization.

Culture is one of those things that you just feel, even if it's hard to define. Values enable you to attract like-minded people who want to volunteer and could eventually work as employees in the culture and atmosphere you have created. If you're just starting out, then you may not be at this point to hire yet, but you will be soon enough.

VALUES ARE NOT FOR SALE

Values are the nonnegotiable of the organization. Remembering this will help you make the tough decisions for the future. It will help you shape the identity of your organization, which is especially important as you grow. You don't want to have an identity crisis in the middle of a growth spurt, when you might truly need the money and be tempted to sacrifice your values to get it.

HOW TO CREATE MEANINGFUL AND MEMORABLE VALUES

In case this isn't clear, let me say it again: before you go any further in bringing this vision to life, please, please, please, sit down and determine your values—both personally and for the organization.

Information is coming at us at an increasingly rapid rate. When people started using PowerPoint presentations, they often lasted thirty minutes. Then TED Talks appeared on the scene, and people had to get their point across in seventeen minutes. Now we have Goalcast, a platform that gives you seven minutes. A YouTube ad is lucky to last seven seconds before we are able to select the "Skip the Ad" button. People's available time and attention span are decreasing, so we need to adapt and make our values stand out so people can remember them.

I recommend limiting your values to five. We started off with twelve, but people couldn't remember them. I even had a hard time keeping them straight, and I created them! I have been known to give pop quizzes to make sure people know our values; it's that important. When we had twelve values, those pop quizzes would leave me frustrated, because only one person out of ten would get them all right. So, my board and I went back to the drawing board and narrowed our values down to five meaningful and memorable ones.

Teach adherence to the values above programs and fundraising.

If your team remembers, acts, and makes decisions based on those values—in other words, if *everyone* is using the same moral compass—then you, as the founder, should be able to breathe a little easier knowing that you don't have to be everywhere or do everything. Teach adherence to the values above programs and fundraising. If you put your organizational values above all else, you are on your way to creating a purpose-driven organization that will continue to thrive long after you and the founding members are gone.

One point to remember about values: if they don't make you at least a little uncomfortable, they're not the right ones. Values go against the grain and help you make the hard decisions. They create the defining moments you will face as a leader, when you will have to slide the $10,000 check back across the table.

START WITH I

When you start considering values, you have to know what *you* believe before you can answer any questions about what your organization stands for. Your values have to start with "I" before they can switch to "we."

Really, there can't be a "we" if you don't believe what's coming out of your mouth.

In the early days of Roc Solid Foundation, one of my mentors told me that he answers three simple questions once a year, to help him truly know himself and to stay on track. He suggested that I answer them as well, and now I believe every leader should take time to answer these three key questions:

1. Who am I?
2. Where am I going?
3. What do I believe?

You know what I'm going to say next: pull out your journal and answer these questions. Before you can lead an organization, you have to know who you are, where you're going, and what you stand for. Who you are is far more important than what you'll ever do as the leader and founder. As you think and write, ask yourself this bonus question: "What do I want to be known for when all is said and done?"

Here's another exercise. Write the statement "I believe _____" and make a list of your core beliefs. It's okay to be vague at first, but after your first round, I challenge you to add a few more details.

The following is my original "I believe" list. My values have evolved and become more precise over time, but the core values are the same:

- I believe family is everything.
- I believe that money isn't all it's cracked up to be.
- I believe people are what eternally matters.
- I believe I'm a great husband and father.
- I believe I'm a great leader who loves relentlessly.
- I believe if I can beat cancer, there is nothing in this world that I can't do.

When you get to the section on Roc Solid's values, notice how the organization values have some similarities to my personal "I believe" statements and values. That's to be expected. You have to believe the organization's values in the same way you believe your own, or they will mean nothing.

Your values have to start with "I" before they can switch to "we."

What do you want out of the one and only life you've been given? I asked myself this question when I was lying in my hammock in Costa Rica. I knew life was bigger than what I had been chasing up to that point. The answer to that question has a lot to do with values, what you consider important and worth pursuing with all you've got.

After you answer these questions for yourself, bring in the "we" of your nonprofit: *Who are we? Where are we going? What do we believe?* The "we" involves the community you're serving, your volunteers, and the people who trust you enough to donate their money.

Brain dump a list of your beliefs, and then decide which ones really fit you and your organization. You might start with twenty-five, but think carefully and whittle that list down to the core values—*your* core values, not something you borrowed or took from Google. Your organization might have values that are similar to another organization's but they should still be uniquely yours.

After you brain dump, group the values that sound similar, prioritize, and then wordsmith so they are simple and memorable. Use language that fits you and your brand, not just corporate America. Every organization is different, just like DNA. For example, if you started this organization in memory of a loved one, imagine them saying the phrase you come up with. Add a little of their personality into the values as well.

Don't be afraid to seek counsel from and brainstorm your values with others. Your board of directors and your core group of leaders can help you sort through your thoughts and begin to refine your values.

Here's an example of how values might be worded and the reasoning behind them. Please don't copy and paste these five. Your organization's values should reflect your personal values and the culture and community connected with your nonprofit. This is an opportunity for you to learn from others, but not copy them, since you can never really copy why people do what they do. Be creative!

1. Start and End with Why

In his book *Start with Why*, Simon Sinek says, "People don't buy what you do; they buy why you do it. And what you do simply proves what you believe."[3] People have to understand why you exist as an organization before they will wrap their hearts around what you do. When I tell the story of Roc Solid Foundation, people often forget that I build playsets, but most remember that I'm a childhood cancer survivor and that I lost two cousins to cancer. That's my why. I started this organization, I build playsets and provide Ready Bags, and I'm writing this book because I lost two cousins to pediatric cancer. That fuels me every single day.

One way this value plays out is that we start every meet-

---

3   Simon Sinek, *Start with Why: How Great Leaders Inspire Everyone to Take Action* (New York: Portfolio, 2009), 78.

ing and every build by going around the circle of staff and volunteers and having every person there say why they are there. We even extended our board of directors meeting so that each member has time to share their why. This is a quick and simple way to create a fresh perspective and identify the various ways each person has been impacted by the hope we provide.

2. Families First, Theirs and Ours

First and foremost, this value refers to the community Roc Solid is called to love and serve. Those families always come first, and our decisions at every level should align with this priority. This is the value that helped me say no to the businessman offering $10,000 with stipulations.

On the walls of our headquarters (which is no longer in my parents' garage!), we have large canvas prints of the children we've built playsets for. When budget season comes around, I have been known to take these photos, set them in the conference room chairs, and talk to them about upcoming financial decisions: "How does this affect *you*?" Yes, it may seem a little crazy, but we need to keep the main thing the main thing, and seeing the faces of those we love and serve helps me do that.

When we first formed our values, this one was simply

"Families First." The emphasis on our own families came about because of how things were going on my own personal home front. On the surface, everything looked great, but on the inside, it was slowly falling apart and becoming extremely challenging. I was working eighty-hour weeks and gone every weekend, and when I finally made it home, I was spent. I often found myself yelling at the kids and wanting to retreat to the couch and disengage from everything and everyone around me. I was so focused on carrying out the mission of Roc Solid Foundation that I started neglecting my own family.

As a result, my wife and I hit a rough patch in our marriage. If you hold a single brick for a short time, it doesn't feel too heavy, but over an extended time it can really weigh you down. That's what happened to my wife. She had been holding the brick of keeping the house together, raising our kids, and supporting my dream, and it became extremely heavy. To be honest, I didn't put her first. At best, I was bringing her leftovers, and she deserved me to be the man she had the courage to marry.

I met with my board and let them know that I needed to spend more time with my family and that we needed to make a shift in how we worded this value. We came to realize that if you're no good at home, you're of no value to Roc Solid Foundation or to the community we are called to love and serve.

What I do for a living is pretty neat. I build playsets for kids fighting cancer, and I get lots of accolades for doing so. However, my kids will not care how many playsets daddy has built if I am not home playing with them. We value families first—the ones God has called us to serve and our very own.

3. Marry the Mission, Not the Model

In my research of nonprofits, I realized that it's easy to get stuck using the same model or program because it has worked in the past. The problem is that circumstances, people, money, and culture change, and what worked in the past may no longer be the best way to solve the problem.

By saying we wanted to marry the mission and not the model, we stated our commitment to focus on our mission to bring hope to kids fighting cancer, even if that meant changing or adding or dropping a program. The truth of what we do will never change, but how we do it might.

4. Respect Simplicity

Over the years, I have heard horror stories of dads and grandpas trying to assemble playsets. I learned from my own experience building the playset for Keith's daughter that it can be a complicated, frustrating, drawn-out process. When we started Roc Solid, we knew we had to figure out how to simplify the build. We needed to find a way for people to come out to one of our sites and change the life of another human in one day, not weeks. Pursuing simplicity helps us remain in a rigid state of flexibility, allowing us to navigate any off-the-wall challenges that are thrown at us. We bend, but never break.

As an organization grows, it is natural to overanalyze and overcomplicate things that used to be simple. With a larger nonprofit, you have more team members, and therefore more ideas and opinions. Also, the more people involved, the more opportunities for mistakes to be made. In correcting mistakes, you might insert a quick fix that becomes a new process that slows down the ship. You have to fight to keep things simple.

5. Focus on the People and the Money Will Come

When I was the Chief Everything Officer back in the beginning, the best donation I ever received was eighty-three cents. I was sitting under one of the tents in the front yard at our seventh or eighth build, and this kid rode his Razor scooter past my table several times, curious to see what was going on and obviously trying to get my attention. Unfortunately, I was busy responding to emails and basically ignored him.

Finally, after about twenty minutes, the boy stopped and asked, "What are you doing?"

"We're building a playset for a little girl fighting cancer," I said, and went back to my cell phone.

The boy rode away. About fifteen minutes later, he walked up the street with an older woman and stopped in front of me. He dumped seventy-three pennies and a dime on the table and said, "I want to help the little girl fight cancer."

I put my cell phone down and looked up at him and then the woman, who had tears in her eyes. This kid had drained his piggy bank. He gave everything he had to help this little girl, and I hadn't given him the time of day.

I leaned forward and gave the boy the Roc Solid hat I was wearing, and then I gave him a tour of the build site. I treated him like a million-dollar donor.

That's the day I learned the importance of focusing on people, even the little guy who only has eighty-three cents to give.

Prior to that event, we had the value of focusing on people over profits. But values are something to be fine-tuned over time, and this kid exposed a major missing element in one of our core values, and man did it hurt. I had treated this young kid like crap, yet he still gave me everything he had. It's because of that boy that I came up with one of our power statements: treat everyone like a million-dollar donor. The most important capital in any organization is its people, especially at the beginning, when you don't have money and all you have is people.

This value is also my sales team's mission statement. Above all else, they focus on the people—they treat each one like a million-dollar donor—and they trust the money will come.

HOW TO HELP PEOPLE REMEMBER YOUR VALUES

To get people to remember your values, you have to talk about them often. Tell a story to illustrate them and ask your team members and volunteers to do the same. For example, randomly ask people to tell you about a time when they _____ [insert the value]. My story at the beginning of the chapter illustrates a time when I put families first. Each person on my staff has their own stories around our values, something to make them personal and memorable.

Another way to help people remember your values is to put them into something people will see and use. For example, we give customers, staff members, and volunteers a frame with our five values inside. We also make T-shirts out of our values so people won't forget them.

You can also have a little fun with it. When I see one of my team members living out one of our values, I reward them for being "caught doing good," just like in grade school. Even if the reward is something silly like a Blow Pop or a ten-dollar Starbucks gift card, everyone likes to be acknowledged for doing great work. No one has ever told me to stop telling them how awesome they are doing.

JUST DO IT

If you get your values right from the start, it will make all of your commitments to your business and clients stronger. It will make the people around you better. It will make the community you serve better. It will make your mission stand firm against time. After you're gone, your organization will stay true to the values you believe in.

If you're not willing to endure the pain of thinking through and creating values, don't waste your time creating them. You will face a few gut punches that will test your values. That's business. You need to know who you are and what you stand for before the punches come, or you and your organization will get knocked out.

Values are not a one-time event. They're not something

you create, write on your walls, and forget. They should become part of your DNA, something that is unique to you and your organization.

If I had accepted that $10,000 check, I believe Roc Solid wouldn't be where it is today. We now deploy thousands of Ready Bags to families all over the United States through more than seventy hospital partners. None of that would have been possible if I had not established my values and stuck to them.

After your foundation, program, and values are in place, it's time to find like-minded volunteers to help you carry your mission.

Chapter 5

PIZZA, BEER, AND T-SHIRTS CAN CHANGE THE WORLD

To say I was nervous the day we built Jillian's playset would be a drastic understatement. I was scared to death. This was our very first build. We planned the project, bought the supplies, and lined up about nine friends and family members to help, but I was still petrified it would fail. When I woke up to pouring rain that morning, I breathed a huge sigh of relief. This was the excuse I was looking for to call off the project.

I picked up the phone and called my buddy, John. "Hey, I think we need to cancel this project. It's pouring and there is no way we can build. Plus who's going to show up anyway?"

"What are you talking about?" John said. "I'm already in your garage. I've put up the tents. I've laid out pallets for people to walk on. We are building this playset, one way or another, so get your butt up and get out here."

Resisting my fears, I finally walked outside. It was nearly hurricane status. Tree limbs were scattered throughout the yard and my driveway had puddles so deep you could fish in them. But John was not discouraged. He already had a game plan for how to set up my yard, so I started shuffling tables, moving coolers, and changing batteries in the drills, even though I really thought we were wasting our time. I didn't think anyone was going to show, and I kept expecting texts from my friends wanting to bail.

The excuses never came; the complete opposite actually. I received texts and phone calls asking if people could bring their friends. I was the only one making excuses trying to sabotage this project.

By six o'clock that night, there was a crowd of people standing under the tents, which were irrelevant at that point because the rain was coming in from the sides and rising from the bottom. I used to pay people good money to work on days like this, and they wouldn't show up, and here I had around thirty people standing in the pouring rain to build a playset for free.

"How the hell did you get all these people to show up?" asked Jerry, my first chairman. We were standing on my porch, getting ready to kick off the build.

"I haven't the slightest clue," I said with a smile. "And to tell you the truth, I don't know what to do next."

"You brought all these people here for one thing, one thing only...build a playset for a little girl. So let's just do what we signed up to do. Eric, when your idea of building playsets for every child fighting cancer takes off, the rain is going to be the least of your problems."

I took a deep breath, stepped off my front porch, and walked into the center of the group. At that moment I realized that this had nothing to do with me. It had everything to do with the people in that circle and the beautiful little girl who would be receiving a new playset the next day.

I don't remember what I said, but it didn't really matter. Despite the terrible weather conditions, people stayed. We broke up into teams and built the playset in sections. Around midnight we put the larger pieces of the playset together and loaded the set onto a trailer to transport it to Jillian's house early the next morning. We were exhausted and wet, but we were also united and excited. We gave hugs and high fives and headed home. As I fell asleep, I wondered if anyone would show up since five o'clock was only a few hours away.

I didn't need to worry. When I walked out my front door the next morning, the same crowd was there standing in my driveway wearing their "I Am Roc Solid" T-shirts, ready for the big day.

When we arrived at Jillian's house around five thirty in the morning, it was still dark. Due to all the excitement, we never stopped to think about what time the sun comes up.

We waited for the sky to lighten and then got to work. Around eight o'clock, Jillian and her mom left the house for a mommy-daughter date chauffeured by my buddy Brian. We figured we had around three hours to assemble the playset while Jillian and her mom ate breakfast and had their nails done. The pressure was real! Not only had I never done this before, it was still cold and rainy, which added to the challenge.

Despite all the uncertainties and stumbling blocks, we completed the assembly ahead of schedule and eagerly awaited Jillian's return. The skies cleared, and the sun decided to show up just in time. Every person who had worked on the playset stood in the family's backyard, waiting to see Jillian's reaction to the gift they worked so hard to give her. The rain. The exhaustion. The tears and fears. This was it, the moment we all had been waiting for.

When Jillian rounded the corner and saw her playset for the first time, we all saw firsthand the impact of what we had just done. We gave Jillian a piece of her childhood and allowed her to be a kid and forget about cancer for a few minutes. When I looked at the bunch of ordinary people who accomplished this extraordinary feat, despite their lack of experience and the less-than-ideal conditions, I realized that it doesn't take much to get people to give their time and talent to help another human being. People want to do good. They want to be involved. They want to see the direct impact.

When you give people a common purpose to rally behind and throw in a free T-shirt, a few slices of pizza, and some beer, you really can change the world.

The volunteers are the heartbeat of what keeps any nonprofit going. They are what you will build your community on in the years to come. In this chapter, we'll look at the importance of creating a story that volunteers want to be part of and how to keep those people coming back for more.

RECRUIT

After you develop the program and acquire the practical pieces, whatever they are—playset design, parts, tools, socks, suits, and so on—you need to recruit volunteers to bring it all together.

Recruiting starts with having a clearly defined mission that people understand. Remember that mission statement you created to file for 501(c)(3) status? Here's another reason for having one. People won't give their time and talent to your mission if they don't understand what you're doing.

**If you capture their attention,
you capture their time.**

To successfully recruit volunteers, you also need to create a story that captures their attention. If you capture their attention, you capture their time.

CREATE THE STORY

One day I was in Home Depot picking up supplies. Right in front of me stood a guy wearing a "I Am Roc Solid" T-shirt. I could hardly control my excitement. I tapped him on the shoulder and asked, "Hey, where'd you get that T-shirt?"

The guy set down the smaller items he was holding so he could tell me the story properly. "Oh man, let me tell you. I helped put together a playset for a little guy fighting cancer a couple weeks ago. When he came running around the corner and saw it...man, it was so awesome. The guy who started Roc Solid quit his job, sold everything he had, and now he's building playsets all over the world for these kids!"

He made me sound like I was six foot ten and bulletproof. I didn't have the courage to tell him that the five-foot-eight and slightly husky guy standing in front of him was that founder. I felt like it would destroy the rest of his day. Plus, I liked his idea of me much better.

T-shirts are one way to invite people into the story you have created. The guy at Home Depot was so excited about sharing the impact moment when the boy ran around the corner. He clearly felt part of changing that little guy's life and had a wonderful memory of that day. Favorite T-shirts become favorite because of the feeling and memory attached to them.

A bonus is that when people wear your apparel, you get free advertising when someone asks about the shirt and the person wearing it explains where they got it.

My hope is that volunteers take it a step further and

invite others to be part of the experience. One of our volunteer leaders was wearing his Roc Solid T-shirt in a paint store when a lady tapped his shoulder and asked what the shirt meant. Tommy shared his experience and invited her to participate, and she ended up becoming a top volunteer in the organization for three years. People want to do good, and your T-shirt may be the invitation they need.

Before you invite people into your story, however, you have to create it. You have to design an experience that allows volunteers to participate in your purpose, whether it's feeding people living on the streets or building a playset for a child fighting cancer. If you give people a hands-on experience in which they can see and feel how lives are being changed by their involvement, they will keep coming back. Give them experiences to share with others. Give them a reason to pull out their phone and take a photo. People repeat stories they are personally connected to, so we simply need to create those stories and invite people to join us.

There are three main parts to any story: people (the characters), place (the setting), and purpose (the mission or meaning). In creating a hands-on experience, your organization has two main characters: the community you serve and the volunteers. It's easy to focus on the first main character; after all, they are the reason for the mission. However, it's important to keep your volunteers in mind, too. Create an experience that shows you have thought about them and value their presence.

For example, parents who wake up at six in the morning every day to get their children out of bed and out the door might not want to join a volunteer opportunity on Saturday morning at seven. Can you start at eight thirty, let the Mama Bear sleep in a little, and still accomplish your mission? In addition, many people are nervous to volunteer for the first time. It takes courage for someone to show up to a random location with a bunch of random people. Make it easy for people to locate the volunteer opportunity and jump in. Have the cones out or flags flying so they know that they are in the right location. Make sure parking is available and that people know where to park. Think through every aspect of your volunteers' experience and prepare for each part. Doing so makes a huge difference in whether or not they come back.

ASK

Another mantra I live by: the answer is always no if you don't ask. It holds true for asking people to join your board of directors, finding people to fight with you in the trenches, finding donors, and recruiting volunteers.

That first build for Jillian happened by word of mouth.

TOOLS TO HELP SHARE THE STORY

Whenever you share on your website and social media that you're looking for volunteers, always include a photo or video. For example, we might say, "Great opportunity to help another human being. Interested?" and then include a photo of a child on a swing or a group of volunteers building a playset. Use the photo to ask the question and to show the direct impact the volunteer will be making.

One note on wording: We don't use the word need when we post about volunteer opportunities; it sounds too negative. We emphasize the positive: a chance to help another person. For example, rather than say, "We need volunteers to help build this playset," we say, "We have an amazing opportunity for you to come and build a playset."

The volunteer construction crew consisted of my family and their close friends, and they came simply because we asked. Many returned for later builds because they had an excellent experience seeing Jillian play, knowing they had a part in that, and it didn't hurt that we had free beer, pizza, and T-shirts. (As you can probably guess, an excellent experience doesn't happen by accident. It requires preparation; more on that shortly.)

Besides people you know personally, you can also recruit volunteers at local social associations, like Rotary and Lions Clubs. They meet on a regular basis and are always looking for ways to better their communities, so they often invite nonprofits to speak and share their mission. Schools are another great place to recruit because the majority of them require community service as part of graduation requirements.

Whenever you visit these clubs or schools, don't go empty-handed. I encourage you to bring swag, brochures, and anything you can leave behind that will help them remember you. If you're standing at the table when people pick up swag, put that elevator pitch and power statement of yours to use.

ENGAGE

After you successfully recruit volunteers, your next task is to engage them more fully in what you're doing, both during the volunteer experience and beyond. The best way to do that is to make each volunteer feel seen and heard.

START AND END WITH WHY

At the beginning of every build, we gather the volunteers and ask them to briefly share why they came. Some people are "voluntold" by a spouse or a boss. Some accompany a friend. Some knew someone with cancer and this is their way of paying it forward. You never know the reason behind people's actions unless you ask.

At the end of every build, as we're loading the last tools,

we ask volunteers to share their favorite part of the experience. One might say, "I loved it when Jillian came running around the corner," or "I loved the rush of thinking we were not going to make the timeline and somehow we did." Many times, a parent will speak about enjoying time with family and showing their kids they can make a difference.

Try this at the start and finish of each project, and you'll see the impact that has been made on your volunteers. You'll also start to build relationships that will help you engage volunteers and grow your program. Make sure you keep this time positive. There is always room for improvements, but we try to end all projects and events on a positive note.

BE PREPARED

For any project, make sure you're prepared. You wouldn't invite people over for Thanksgiving dinner without doing the shopping, cooking the meal, setting the table, and having the dishes washed and ready. The same is true of inviting people to participate in your experience. Be ready when they arrive. Have the swag set up, the waivers out, the supplies ready to go, and your opening words rehearsed. Be prepared to give your volunteers an unforgettable experience that they will rave about to family and friends.

One of the best compliments Roc Solid regularly receives is, "Man, you guys have thought of everything." That means we are prepared and ready to host our amazing volunteers. It means we value their time just as much as we value their money.

KEEP IT SIMPLE

People are busy. They're giving their time, which is already limited, so help them feel like they are getting the most out of what time they give you.

The program should not be complicated; we like to say that anyone with a sixth-grade education should be able to do it. Volunteers who have never touched a drill should be able to participate in a build. We want to make it simple and enjoyable so that people leave our project in a timely manner and feel like they played an active role in positively changing the life of another human being.

Keeping it simple took a lot of testing and pivoting. Whenever we realized something wasn't simple, we changed it and tested it again. We even went as far as weighing the drills to make sure a six-year-old could hold it long enough to get a screw in. If your organization packs care packages for people living on the street, you might make a list of all the supplies and pack the bags over and over to make sure the items fit in the bag properly. You might label the bins of items so volunteers don't have to guess which box they should pull out. Paying attention to the small details will help you streamline your process and keep it simple.

KEEP IT FUN

As mentioned earlier, setting is part of the story you are creating, and you want that environment to be comfortable so people want to return. In other words, keep it fun! Turning your pain into your purpose doesn't have to be a heavy burden. It's okay to laugh while you work; in fact, I encourage it. In addition to being the best medicine, laughter breaks down walls, creates relationships, and brings positivity.

When volunteers would help us in our office, which is down the street from a 7-Eleven, I've been known to stop everything and march the whole group down to the convenience store for their choice of candy and a Slurpee. I've also brought rotisserie chicken and beer to packing sessions for an impromptu picnic. Be like Michael Scott from *The Office* and have some good old-fashioned, awkward fun!

To create a truly fun atmosphere, it helps to know your audience. For example, we had a group of Mama Bears volunteer to pack Ready Bags, and each of them had a child with cancer. As they walked in we handed them a glass of wine. After they sat down, we walked around with a basket so they could drop in their cell phones and be "off the grid" for a little while. We catered to them all afternoon, providing cheese and crackers, refilling wine glasses, and giving them space to have adult conversation with other Mama Bears.

BRING THE SWAG

People love free stuff, and honestly, it's the least you can do to "pay" your volunteers. People don't give their time or talent for the free stuff, but it is a great way to keep them coming back.

When people show up for a build, they sign their waivers and pick up their T-shirt. We tell them they can take the T-shirt home or put it on right away, and we have a clean space shuttle (aka porta potty) available for them to do so. Most people put it on. This is key because we live in a selfie nation. We want volunteers wearing their swag so that when they're taking pictures and posting them to social media, our mission is being broadcasted. This involves them in our story; it's part of a great experience.

FOLLOW UP

After each build, my leadership team and I take time to

recognize the volunteers on our social media platforms. We also give them a thank-you call and send a hand-written note. Following up in various forms is crucial to engaging volunteers in what you're doing.

If we made an emotional connection with a certain volunteer, we make sure that follow-up call happens within seventy-two hours. We thank them for coming and invite them back. Seventy-two hours is the key window, because after that the emotional charge fades and the busyness of life starts to creep back in.

Now we have branded cards, but in the beginning, I went to the dollar store and bought note cards close to our brand color. We have found that when people return for a second or third build, they often tell us about the thank-you note posted on their refrigerator. People really do appreciate receiving a piece of mail that's not a bill. Little things like that contribute to the overall experience as well. Thanking your volunteers lets them know that the giving of their time and talents does not go unnoticed.

ASK FOR FEEDBACK

Don't be afraid to ask people for feedback after they have participated in one of your projects. What you hear may hurt, because you've poured your heart and soul into bringing this vision to life, but don't skip this step. Honor the feedback. Be willing to address it and make changes. Contrary to popular opinion, the customer isn't always right, but you have to be willing to receive feedback and take action if it's valid to advancing the mission. You create buy-in when volunteers give feedback and see action, and when you get buy-in, volunteers show up again and again.

Truett Cathy, founder of Chick-fil-A, once said, "If you focus on getting better, it will be mandatory that you get bigger."[4] Those words have allowed me to receive feedback, both positive and negative, because getting bigger allows us to bring hope to more kids fighting cancer.

RETAIN

Recruiting and engaging volunteers is the path to your ultimate goal: keeping them. If you retain your amazing volunteers, your organization is more likely to experience growth, and you will build the team that will help you continue to love and serve your community.

BECOME AN EXPERT AT SAYING THANK YOU

Yes, I'm repeating myself. Saying thank you is how you engage volunteers, and it's also how you retain them.

Whether you send a card, make a phone call, send a text, or do all of the above, become an expert at thanking every person who shows up to help. Gratitude is a currency that we can spend without the fear of bankruptcy. The outcome of your organization depends on the effort you place in learning this habit.

Gratitude is also an unscheduled, unexpected blessing to someone else. How many of you have received that phone call or that text message at just the right moment? The person's words may have helped you make an important decision that you had been thinking or praying about, or they may have arrived on a day when you were feeling like no one appreciated you. With a heartfelt thank-you, we have the opportunity to be a part of that blessing for someone else. Expressing gratitude takes minutes out of our day, but the impact creates ripples that extend far into the future.

Gratitude is a currency that we can spend without the fear of bankruptcy.

I have never had a volunteer leave our organization because we were too over-the-top with gratitude. However, I have heard of people leaving because they did not feel appreciated.

Get in the habit of thanking the people you are serving, too. Thank the guy living on the street because he allowed you to give him socks. Thank the family of the child with cancer. Thank the couple who allowed you to repair their credit. Whoever your community is, get in the habit of thanking them.

Whenever we finish a build, I thank the family for letting a group of random strangers show up in their yard at five thirty in the morning. I thank them for trusting us. I usually tell them that I don't know if trusting us makes them crazy or smart, but I thank them nonetheless. No matter how much success you have, you can never forget the power of a thank-you.

When I worked in construction, I rarely thanked my employees. I figured a paycheck was enough. It wasn't. During that time in my life, they were a means to the end of fattening my pockets so I could buy more stuff. I expected nonstop work from my employees, and I wasn't thankful for it, and that likely contributed to the loss of my construction business.

If you keep a thankful heart, give thanks without a promise of return, and remain grateful for the smallest things, your organization will be a force to be reckoned with. Remember: a thank-you is the volunteer's paycheck, and it goes a long way.

Get creative in your thank-yous, and make sure they

fit your mission. A handwritten note is wonderful, but if someone helps you repeatedly, you might want to increase the thank-you ante a little. For a repeat volunteer at a soup kitchen, buy a gold ladle and have a special message engraved on it. We cut up pieces of an old play-set, and write notes on them with a Sharpie.

A thank-you is the volunteer's paycheck.

Give gifts that pass the "fired" test. In other words, if someone had your gift displayed in their office at work, is it something they would take with them if they got fired, as opposed to dumping it in the trash on their way out the door? If it is important to them, your gift will end up on their next desk, so make it worthy not only of display, but also of explanation. Even your thank-you gifts should be part of the story and experience that leave a lasting impression.

THREE-YEAR CYCLE

Over the last twelve years, I've seen volunteers come and go in approximately three-year cycles. Life happens, people get busy, and priorities shift, so you need to be constantly recruiting and engaging new volunteers.

People often find refuge in volunteering. During their first year, people become familiar with the organization, make sure their values align with yours, and take something away from the experience. They continue volunteering if they find value in their contribution to your mission.

If you engage volunteers as I've suggested, by saying thank you and seeking feedback, they often remain and grow in leadership during their second year of involvement. This is when they really flourish. They become invested and start to lead other volunteers and can be trusted to live out the mission. They are typically the first to arrive and last to leave. The second year is the real sweet spot.

During the third year, we find many people engage in about half as many projects, and then it decreases even further. It's not that they're turning their back on the mission; their lives simply change. If you've been an expert at saying thank you and engaging them on a personal level, they often come back when life calms down. This is tough advice to follow, but I'll say it anyway: don't take it personally when people step away. It's not all about you. Life just happens.

For the first four years, I did not receive a paycheck from Roc Solid. When we finally reached a financially stable point and the board approved a salary for me, we unfortunately experienced a major volunteer culture shift. Some of our main contributors, who had given their blood, sweat, and tears, could not believe I took a paycheck, and they mutinied. We went from around twenty-five volunteers to seven.

You never know when something like this might happen, either because of disagreements, differences of opinion, or evolving life events. It may sting a little, but it is nothing compared to what the community of people you are called to love and serve are experiencing. That's why you need to continually fill that volunteer pipeline through recruiting and engaging people who believe in your mission.

VOLUNTOLD TO VOLUNTEER

Many people come to their first project because they were "voluntold" to go. One family—husband, wife, and son—showed up, and the husband's demeanor suggested he had been voluntold to participate. I tried to engage the man with small talk, but he had more important things happening on his phone—until he noticed I was teaching his son how to drill. I'm not sure what changed, but he put his phone away and began to help. This father-son duo became the best builders on site.

At the end of the day, I walked up to this father and son. I knelt down so I was eye level with the boy and said, "You did amazing today. You're the VIP of the build site, and

I want you to have this special patch. You are what hope looks like." I looked up and tears were streaming down his dad's face.

Don't be discouraged if voluntold people show up. You never know who will be touched by the mission and experience a shift in heart and mind, from being *made* to participate to *choosing* to be involved. I've seen this shift happen countless times, and watching it happen never gets old. Keep reaching out, keep engaging, and you'll see disengaged family members, employees forced into "fun" team building, and people doing court-appointed charity work find common ground in giving back and become wholeheartedly engaged in what you're doing.

TIME AND TALENT

Although you may have had the idea for your nonprofit, its success is ultimately tied to your volunteers. You need people to join your mission, to give their time and talents to help you carry it out. To truly engage and retain those volunteers, you must become an expert in saying thank you. You must give them an experience they will want to share with others and that allows them to see, feel, and touch the difference they're making in people's lives.

Keeping your pipeline of volunteers will be challenging at times, but the effort will always be worth it. You'll be amazed how little things like pizza, beer, and T-shirts can help you change the world.

Chapter 6

BEYOND THE GOLF TOURNAMENT

Although selling Krispy Kreme donuts successfully funded our first build for Jillian, I didn't think that would work as a long-term fundraising plan for my nonprofit. I began to research what other nonprofits were doing, and one of the first ideas I came across was hosting a golf tournament. So, a golf tournament it was!

During the planning process, one of my buddies sent me a list of the fundraising golf tournaments going on within a hundred-mile radius. There were *two hundred*. These tournaments were essentially happening every other day, and we had to somehow fit ours in on a day that wasn't already taken by another organization. The only day remaining was a Tuesday in the middle of winter.

Still, I ignored the writing on the wall and threw a golf tournament because, according to my research, that's what you did if you were a nonprofit. I figured there must be a reason golf tournaments were so popular among nonprofits, so why fix it if it's not broken, right? After six months of planning, tracking down entry fees and hole sponsorships, and watching the weather nonstop, our golf tournament ended up being a successful event, and we actually raised around $10,000.

I am grateful for the funds raised, all the golfers who showed up, and the volunteers who busted their butts to host this tournament. Still, I couldn't shake the thought that we had simply blended in with every other nonprofit. Kids with cancer deserve better. Plus, less than 10 percent of the people who participated could tell me the cause they were playing for. I didn't know many of the players, so I stood on the tee box and asked a group of the golfers if they knew about the organization they were supporting and what they did. One person said Habitat for Humanity and another said they feed the homeless.

My experience throwing that one golf tournament set me on a mission to find creative ways to raise money for Roc Solid Foundation. Fundraising in unique ways takes imagination and resourcefulness, but the payoffs are worth it.

You've spent hours thinking about your problem, solution, and program. You've narrowed down your mission and created clear, powerful statements to describe it. You've labored over your values for the organization. Don't stop now! Put that same amount of effort into finding the fundraising options that work best for your organization, your mission, and your audience.

WHY NOT A GOLF TOURNAMENT

In case you've never participated in a golf tournament fundraiser, let me paint the scene: Everyone gathers together, they check in with registration, and then depending on time of day, they grab either breakfast or lunch and grub it down so quickly that half of them have to pop Tums by hole three. Then they make a beeline for their golf carts, and a golf pro from the course takes five minutes to outline the rules. At the end of his talk, almost as an afterthought sometimes, the pro says, "Oh, here's So and So Founder from Nonprofit X who is hosting this event." Then So and So will get a chance to speak from a microphone with terrible feedback, but no one's really listening anyway because they're anxious to get on the course and show off their Tiger Woods swing. People come to a golf tournament to play golf, socialize, and frequently take advantage of the free booze. They don't come to hear So and So speak.

At our first golf tournament fundraiser, I spoke for fifteen minutes and made everyone angry. I believed it was the right time to capture everyone's heart to change the world. Man, was I wrong. It was way too long. Quick tip: if you ever speak at a golf tournament, keep it under two minutes, so you don't get death stares when all the carts leave for their tee boxes. Here's another situation where elevator pitches and power statements really come in handy!

Let me be clear: golf tournaments are not bad. If you can find other people to throw a golf tournament for you, go for it. But planning and throwing golf tournaments yourself may not be the best investment of your already-limited time and resources. Here are several reasons why:

Golf tournaments blend in. If you want to be an organization that stands out, throwing fundraisers like everyone else is not the way to go. Plus there's always a big-hitter nonprofit throwing a golf tournament, and you'll be competing for a decent day and course. Don't settle for a Tuesday in the middle of winter.

Planning a golf tournament takes a lot of time and resources. Yes, I'm repeating myself because this is key, especially when you're first starting. If you're still working a full-time job, you're already spread too thin. Do you really have the time and energy to hunt down sponsors and golfers, buy goodies for the gift bags, put the bags together, run to the printer to pick up the hole sponsor signs, get the petty cash for the raffle tickets, and make the last-minute stop for a raffle item you forgot?

Outdoor events are risky. What if it rains the day of your golf tournament? You lose money. Many golf courses and caterers require a nonrefundable deposit. When you're starting, you don't have money to lose. Even now that Roc Solid is established, we try to limit outdoor events. The risk must be worth the reward to gamble with Mother Nature.

You have a limited number of asks. In the fundraising world, you have only so many asks each year, and you can burn through them pretty quickly when your database of donors is small. The people who support your mission and love you unconditionally can only give so much, and as you venture beyond that group, you need to be strategic about who you ask and when. Because planning a golf tournament involves a lot of asking—to get sponsors, golfers, donations for goody bags, and more—you end up burning through your asks in one shot, for very little in return.

For example, you could ask someone to come volunteer at the soup kitchen, or purchase a suit, or take you up on a hole sponsorship at your golf tournament, but probably not all three. Why not ask someone to buy $150 worth of men's ties or Lego sets instead of asking them for a plastic sign that's going to get thrown away at the end of the golf tournament? To me, that seems like a much smarter use of your asks.

It's harder to generate leads. In addition to raising money, nonprofits hold fundraisers to generate leads for future events and fundraisers. At a golf tournament, people are scattered all over the course, so it's more difficult to make these connections.

You miss your opportunity to talk about the mission. Again, people come to a golf tournament to play golf. If you try to fit in your mission connection at the beginning, you have about two minutes, and people are barely listening anyway. If you try to connect at the end, you're often talking to a half-empty room since people typically leave as soon as they finish the last hole. Out of the hundred golfers who attended our first tournament, about thirty stayed for the after-party where I talked about the mission. That's not a sustainable fundraising model.

SO, YOU DECIDED TO THROW
A GOLF TOURNAMENT

Maybe you've already started planning your first fundraiser, and it's a golf tournament. I don't blame you. That's what all the "experts" recommend. That's what I did.

Here are a few suggestions to create a unique experience for the participants and make the most of your opportunities to share your mission.

Display your mission. Put a visual display of your mission at one of the holes, and make sure every golfer hears your elevator pitch before they tee off. For example, at one golf tournament I put a prebuilt playset by the first tee box, and then personally made sure every golfer who came through knew exactly who the tournament was supporting. Seeing the playset gave participants an opportunity to see, touch, and feel that play defeats cancer.

Give a prize to those who stay. Offer a prize to be awarded at the end of the after-party. It can't be a bag of cookies. It has to be something big enough to motivate people to stay when they'd rather leave. A prize valued at $300 to $500 usually does the trick.

During the after-party, have someone talk about your mission, preferably someone who has benefitted from it, like a child or parent that has already been gifted a playset.

Talk to the team captains. Find out who is leading each foursome and call them ahead of time to thank them for participating and let them know about the prize at the end. In addition, give them a challenge. For example, "At the first hole we're going to be telling you about the mission. Between holes 1 and 5, ask your buddies to consider making a contribution to Roc Solid to push the mission forward. I'll even give you the talking points. They'll be in your golf goody bag." You could also create another prize for the person in each foursome who raises the most money.

WHAT TO DO INSTEAD

So, if not a golf tournament, then what? Here are a few suggestions for fundraising in a way that's true to your mission, your organization, and your audience.

GALA

After golf tournaments, the second most popular fundraising event is a gala. Here, you typically serve a meal, have some kind of program, and offer opportunities to participate in your mission. Galas can be very effective *if* you include the element of surprise. If you follow the same program and serve the same rubber chicken year after year, people will lose interest and you'll lose donors.

How do you include the element of surprise? The options are really endless. The key is to create a gala that is unique to your nonprofit and incorporates your mission in every aspect.

Every year we pick a different theme, usually related to children and the power of play. Then we build the gala program around that theme. One year our theme was "What if?" At the end of my presentation, I said, "*What if* we build a playset right now..." I asked everyone to lift their salad plates. Those who found a golden ticket went to the left side of the auditorium, where we fitted them with hard hats and tool belts over their dresses and tuxedos. While the ticket holders assembled the play-set pieces, nonparticipants snapped photos and posted positive feedback on social media, suffering from FOMO (fear of missing out) the whole time.

Once the pieces were completed, we moved them to the center of the room and assembled the final product. A family who had previously received a playset came on stage to speak about the impact that Roc Solid had made on their lives. Then I inserted the element of surprise. Every year we invite one family as a VIP guest. We invited this family on stage, and then announced that they were receiving the playset the audience had just built. The little guy fighting cancer ran to the playset and went headfirst down the slide. Everyone in the room could see and feel the excitement and surprise. They all became a part of that family's story and wrapped their hearts around the hope we build for children fighting cancer.

Another year I asked a nine-year-old cancer fighter, Allison, to be my date to the gala. Beforehand, I visited Allison in the hospital and learned that she loved to draw dresses. I asked her to draw one for me and then passed it on to a local dress designer. Together, they created a dress from one of Allison's very own drawings. During the fitting, Allison was treated like royalty and we recorded the whole experience. We showed the video at the gala, and then I asked the audience to rise for the guest of honor.

Allison came out wearing the dress she had created. She was glowing. Everyone in that audience could see, touch, and feel the hope we provided for her and her family.

While we were in the process of planning another event, I caught wind of a little boy with terminal cancer named Derek. We didn't have time to build Derek a playset, but we were able to give him play in a different form. We found out that he loved everything Nerf, as well as Navy SEALs and the police, so we set up a special Nerf gun fight at a local laser tag place. Derek the Defender received a police escort from his house to the field of battle, where he was greeted by nine Navy SEALs who surrounded Derek's wheelchair and cleared each room of all the imaginary bad guys. Derek's friends and family were all there, as well as local fire departments and people from the community.

At some point during that epic event, someone threw out the idea that it would be cool to have the world's largest Nerf gun fight. I was intrigued and started exploring that possibility.

At our gala a few months later, our guest speaker was Derek's father, who gave a tribute to Derek the Defender, who had lost his battle with cancer a couple weeks earlier. Afterwards, I announced, "Ladies and gentlemen, we have a surprise for you. We are going to attempt to break a world record in Derek's honor."

At that point, our team came forward carrying buckets of Nerf guns and handed them out. Volunteers from six local soccer teams walked in carrying their own Nerf guns and outlined the room where everyone was sitting.

"Here's what we're going to do," I said. "We're going to have a Nerf gun battle for Derek, and in the process we're going to break the world record. We need all 574 guns firing simultaneously and we need to keep it going for seven minutes. Are you game? Ready, set, go!"

Up to that point I had been worried that no one would go for this crazy idea, but my fears quickly disappeared. As the music played, women in stilettos dove across tables, shooting at their husbands. Pregnant ladies ducked under tables and nailed people as they ran by. Guys in tuxedos ran around like Rambo, living out their childhood dreams. As I watched the beautiful mayhem, I thought, *Oh my God, this is working!*

Not only did we break the world record, but when ticket sales opened for our next gala, they sold out in twenty-four hours. That's what the element of surprise can do. It can turn an otherwise traditional fundraiser into something that captures hearts and involves people in what you're doing. (I should add a disclaimer here. While we were in the process of finishing our paperwork for the *Guinness Book of World Records*, another group broke our record. Although we don't have the title anymore, we still have that moment in honor of Derek the Defender.)

In all three examples, the gala guests became part of the story. They participated in our mission in a way they wouldn't have if the program was always the same, and people ate the same rubber chicken, and I gave the same speech. When they left, hundreds of people shared a story they participated in.

Any fundraising event, even a golf tournament, can have this impact if you add the element of surprise. When you create a gasp moment—when people literally gasp at what they're seeing, feeling, or touching—guests become emotionally connected with your story in a powerful way. You know you've done this when people pull out their phones and take photos because they don't want to forget the moment. Every time they look at the photo, they are reminded of what *they* did with their contribution at the fundraiser—not what your organization did.

Yes, it takes time and effort to create these moments, but it's well worth it. Unlike a golf tournament where a small percentage of people might hear your mission, a unique gala with the element of surprise has the potential to reach hundreds and make a much bigger impact.

PHOTOS, PHOTOS, PHOTOS

When the phones come out to take photos, you know people feel like they're part of a community. This is true of volunteers as well as guests at a gala. In this digital age, people take pictures all the time. Use that to your advantage. Encourage staff and volunteers to take and send photos that capture your mission in action. Sending photos in a group text or posting them to social media takes five minutes, but it can have far-reaching results in making people feel part of something larger than themselves.

Also, encourage people to use certain hashtags when they post photos, and make sure those hashtags are clear. Rather than come up with new hashtags for every event, decide on a few that you will use each time; with consistency, these will become recognizable in the social media world. For example, for every fundraiser and every build, we use three main hashtags: #whathopelookslike, #playdefeatscancer, and #buildhopenomatterwhatnomatterwhere.

PRIVATE EVENTS

Another option is to ask a friend to host a private dinner where people can hear about your organization and mission in a more intimate setting. A private event often takes only a month or two to plan, compared with a golf tournament, which can take six or seven months, or a gala, which can take even longer.

The power of a private event lies largely in selecting the right host. That person has to have a big enough space to make the evening comfortable and inviting. The host should also have influence and connections with people who have giving capacity—in other words, they have available money after paying the monthly bills and they are willing to donate. I don't want to sound snooty; those are simply the rules of engagement. You're having a fundraiser to raise money.

I recommend serving food because it breaks up the awkwardness of the ask, but what you serve depends on your audience. If your friend is inviting their old college roommates who once survived on Hot Pockets and ramen noodles in the dorms, bring out those Hot Pockets and noodles. If your friend is inviting a crowd with more refined tastes, caviar and beef tartare might be more appropriate. Or they can serve something in between. Food and drinks simply bring people together.

I recommend keeping it small—no more than twenty people. I also suggest making it an invitation-only event because people love feeling like they made the VIP list.

The guest list itself should consist of people who have never heard of your organization and have the giving capacity that fits your need. For example, if your goal for the event is $2,000, you might invite twenty people who can make a one-time donation of $100. Know your audience and their giving capacity in terms of your ask.

Be sure to have tangible ways to help explain and sell your mission, for example, photos—lots of photos. A visual like this is a great conversation starter and it gives people the opportunity to see what you're doing. At each person's plate, you might include a "why" photo to show the completion of the mission, the moment the problem is solved. Jason might use a picture of a clean-shaven guy wearing a brand-new suit. Stephanie might use a photo of a couple standing in front of a house, holding a set of keys. Darlene might have a picture of a child holding a finished Lego creation. We use a photo of a young cancer fighter sitting on a swing, smiling from ear to ear. When people arrive, they will see exactly what you're doing and what their involvement in your story will do.

One important note: make sure your host is willing to make a donation commitment and share it with their guests. It applies a little bit of pressure to those who have just received a free meal.

A typical private event fundraiser might go like this: At the beginning of the evening, the host welcomes their guests and allows people to mingle and enjoy appetizers and cocktails. Then dinner is served. After people have eaten and the plates have been cleared, the host stands up and says something like, "Hey, everyone. I brought you all here for a reason. This mission is near and dear to my heart, and I want you to hear from Eric. He can explain the mission and vision better than I can."

At that point, it's your turn. First, *briefly* share what your organization is all about. Remember that elevator pitch and power statement? Use them now!

Then bring in the element of surprise by involving someone who has benefitted from your organization. I often have a Mama or Papa Bear speak, or if the child with cancer is older, I let them take the mic. Sometimes I'll have parents record a video at home and we'll present that if they couldn't appear in person. One time I had the parents of a child we built for serve dinner, and then come up during the program to share their story. It was a powerful way to bring the guests into the mission so they could see, touch, and feel how Roc Solid brings hope to children fighting cancer.

No matter who speaks, make sure they feel comfortable doing so. Don't assume everyone wants to share their story with a crowd of strangers. Ask, and if they say no, honor their response.

If someone is willing to share their story, take time to coach them. Give them a sense of what you're looking for. Don't put words in their mouth, but help them articulate key points in their own way. I give some guidelines around time limits in particular. A good starting point is to keep the speech between seven and twelve minutes. No matter how engaged and how passionate your audience is about the cause, it takes a professional speaker to keep people's attention for over fifteen minutes. The last thing you want is to lose their focus. Lose their focus, lose their money. Even though these private events are fun, you can't forget why you're there: raising funds to help your community.

Have the person record their speech on their phone and then watch it, take a few notes on their delivery, and then record it again. This time, have them send it to you. Make notes on what you see and share them. Be careful not to put your spin on their story. You are just looking for "ums" or little tics that most people never pick up on.

However you do this personal story part, keep it classy. You don't want it to look like you are exploiting a person who has benefited from your mission. At the same time, hearing directly from someone who has benefited from money donated will speak volumes to the guests you're about to ask to give.

After the personal story, take five to ten minutes to wrap up and deliver your ask. Keep your pitch short, and be very direct. Don't leave any room for people to wonder what you are asking. Stay away from saying, "If you feel like giving..." because that sounds too optional. The way I see it there is only one option: give. Be more direct: "Here's an opportunity for you to help someone like the family you just heard from. Would you consider giving

$1,000 to help us continue our mission?" Also, steer clear of using the word *need*. You don't want people to think you're needy or that they're investing in a failing mission. We say "opportunity" instead. Opportunity is positive and life-giving; it brings hope. Who doesn't love new and exciting opportunities?

After your ask, you might say something like, "Would you consider filling out the card that's at your table? I'll be at the front door. You can bring the card to me and ask questions. Thank you so much for coming, and have a wonderful night."

Your whole program—talking about your organization, having someone share, and asking for contributions—should take no more than fifteen minutes. When you're done, take a seat and let your host conclude the evening with an additional ask, for example, "Now you know about this organization that's near and dear to my heart. My wife and I have committed X dollars. Will you consider making a contribution to give play back to kids fighting cancer?"

When the host finishes, have house music playing—not the Sarah McLaughlin, tug-at-your-emotions music, but whatever fits the groove of the group. Then stand near the door so people can't leave without giving you something, whether it's an email address or their business card or a donation. If you are not at the door, make sure someone from your team is and that they are equipped to handle the flow of questions that may come, as well as all types of payments. We take cash, check, or charge.

When you create the purpose, you create the purchase.

My mission statement with private events is when you create the purpose, you create the purchase. When people see that photo, hear that speaker, or watch that video, they become emotionally connected to what you're doing. You can't create that moment at a golf tournament.

TIPS FOR ASKING

Asking for money is hard and uncomfortable, even for me, and I've been doing it for years. Here are a few things to keep in mind, whether you're talking to a group or an individual:

Remind yourself who you're asking for. Every day, write out "I'm not asking for myself. I'm asking for _____" and fill in the blank with the name of someone in your community. I fill in that blank with the names of pediatric cancer fighters I have met. Also, remind yourself, if you're not going to ask on their behalf, who is?

Make a game of asking. For example, each week write down a list of people to reach out to. After each conversation, put their response next to their name: yes or no. My win is not the yes or the money. It's the nos. I've found that it generally takes seven nos to get to a yes, so every no gets me one step closer. Find your algorithm; it might be ten to one or five to one, but look at those nos as wins getting you one step closer to the yes.

Remember that people aren't saying no to you or to the people you're serving. They say no because they may not have the money. They may have lost their job. Their mother-in-law might be moving in with them. You don't know what people are going through. Taking offense to a no is a choice. If you start taking offense, you will never be successful in asking for money. I know because I took offense the first couple of years and stopped asking, which affected the growth of our organization.

Practice, practice, practice. I used to talk to myself in the mirror. I practiced asking over and over. I practiced on the people close to me and requested feedback. I also practiced specific wording: "Would you consider supporting our mission to _____?" rather than "Will you give me _____?"

Follow up, follow up, follow up. The follow-up is just as important as the ask. Many people will commit on site but won't have the capacity to fill the gift at the moment, so you must follow up. It's also a good idea to double-check the potential donor's contact information before they leave. Plus, we've all committed to something in the heat of the moment, and then forgotten about it in a week. Your follow-up will keep their commitment at the forefront of their minds, and their pockets.

I still get nervous about going into meetings to ask for support. What helps me on the day of a big ask is to work out first thing in the morning, because it puts me in the right frame of mind. Then I go to our social media pages and look at the photos of children we've helped over the last twelve years. I review our mission. And I remind myself, "I am not asking for Eric Newman. I am asking for every child fighting cancer. If not me, then who?"

CAMPUS TOUR

One way to show donors where their money is going is to give them a tour of your campus. For example, my campus is a build site, specifically at the end of the build when the child receives the playset. Jason's campus is graduation day when he delivers a suit to someone who has completed the interview training program. Remember to include the element of surprise here, too. For me, the surprise is when the child runs around the corner and sees the playset; for Jason, it's the person walking across the stage, the look of pride clear on his face. In that moment, a potential donor will see, feel, and touch the mission. Even if they've seen a video on your website, there's nothing like experiencing it in person.

The idea of a campus tour came up after I met a dean who gave donors tours of the university campus, strategically timed so that the campus was crowded with students. By doing so, the dean gave the donors a way to see, feel, and touch where their money was going and whom it was benefiting. After the tour, the dean took five minutes to ask the visitors questions like, "What did you find the most impactful? What did you notice?"

You can do the same thing. After giving donors a tour of your campus, find a quiet place to sit and talk to the person about their experience. After you ask for their favorite part, shut up. Don't lead them to tell you what you want to hear. Let them speak.

I believe there is power in the pause. By finding a quiet place and then waiting for the person's response, you give them space to digest what they saw and how they want to help or be a part of it. The next words that come out of the potential donor's mouth are key. They will reveal the next steps they want to take. A quiet place is important because you don't want anyone walking up at that moment, and you don't want to miss what they say because you are too busy speaking.

There is power in the pause.

After they share their thoughts, offer them an opportunity to meet you again to discuss how they can make a financial contribution to move the mission forward. Before they leave, set a date on your calendar. Suggest a few specific dates and locations to meet again. I usually say something like, "Are you available to meet next Monday or Tuesday at the Starbucks on Main Street? I'd love to talk about a potential financial commitment from you and your family."

If they aren't in a position to commit to a meeting right then, that's okay. I usually respond with something like, "No problem. I'll email, call, and text you in the next couple of days to set something up. I really believe you and your family could help us move this mission forward."

Then you must follow through. Send them a text, email, and call reminder—yes, all three!—within forty-eight hours so you catch them while the emotional impact is still fresh.

To have maximum impact, to truly involve people in your story, bring them to ground zero. It's a great way to thank people who are already supporting your mission and to hook potential donors. Ground zero is the story that their money tells.

If you can get people to your campus, 80 percent of your job is done. The hardest part is convincing people to commit their time. Once they are there, the mission will speak for itself. The other 20 percent is follow-up.

DIGITAL FUNDRAISING

If the 2020 pandemic taught us anything about fundraising, it's the importance of having various types of events, including some that do not occur in person. We had already been doing some of the following, but they weren't a priority. Man, has that changed!

Recurring monthly donations are one of the easiest ways for people to donate. They set up a recurring charge on their credit card or a debit card, and that's it. The money automatically comes into your nonprofit every month, providing a steady stream of revenue, which helps with budgeting. Whether someone gives ten dollars or one hundred dollars a month, it goes a long way toward helping you accomplish your mission. It all adds up.

At the beginning of 2019, Roc Solid Foundation had sixty recurring donors. Then the 2020 pandemic hit and we couldn't hold a gala and other in-person events, so we started focusing more on recurring monthly donations. At the beginning of 2021, we had close to three hundred monthly donors, and that number keeps growing.

There are many software options for setting up recurring donations. We have used Neon One and Live Impact, both of which are very easy to use. Most charge fees based on the number of users, so do your research.

When you set up options for monthly donations, make the price points low enough that people can literally set it up and forget about it. I also suggest equating the dollar amount options with something tangible. For example, ten dollars a month over the course of a year will pay for a slide on a playset or twenty-five dollars a month will pay for a new suit at the end of a year. People like to know exactly how their money is helping your mission.

When people commit to monthly donations, it's important to stay in contact with them each month, either by text, email, or newsletter. Share the story of what their money is doing, and be sure to include photos.

Peer-to-Peer Fundraising

Peer-to-peer fundraising involves more strategy and creativity than setting up recurring donations. It uses someone's existing network of friends, family, and social media followers to raise money for a specific event or item in a certain time period. For example, when people run marathons and other races, they often launch peer-to-peer fundraising campaigns that begin the day they start training and end on race day. We have also held peer-to-peer events in which participants have a certain number of weeks to raise enough money to pay for one Ready Bag.

We have seen great success with peer-to-peer fundraising through our social media channels. Start by choosing a giving platform such as Classy.org or Fundly.com. This is where people will make donations and create their own page to share with family and friends. When you research giving platforms, check out the terms and fees.

Some charge a per-transaction fee and others charge a flat rate. I know the fees can leave a bad taste in your mouth, but look at them as a cost of doing business. Without the platforms, you wouldn't be able to receive the money. Find the site that best fits your mission, and make sure the fees don't cause you to lose sleep.

After picking a platform, choose a color theme that matches your brand and then choose an event (for example, a marathon, a concert, or a specific need), determine the length of the campaign, collect some photos and testimonies, set a financial goal, and invite others to join. Spend a little time with each participant to help them set up their own donation page, and then encourage people to share that page with everyone in their social network.

A key part of peer-to-peer fundraising is using social media. Think of it as free advertising. Whenever your nonprofit holds a specific campaign, post it on all your channels, and encourage participants to do the same. Here are a few tips to make the most of your posts:

- Create a sense of urgency: show people the opportunity. For example, if you are running a food bank and your shelves are empty, snap a photo, throw it up on your social channels, and ask for donations.
- Grab their attention: create a short and specific narrative that communicates what the fundraising

campaign is all about. You are competing with a lot of information on the web. Your post needs to stand out and cause people to pause as they are scrolling through social media. For example, we might use a heading like "A hair tie can change the world" and then explain how a hair tie can help a Mama Bear who is spending all day leaning over a hospital bed with her hair falling in her face. The specific ask might be, "Help us provide a hair tie to every Mama Bear with a child fighting for their life."

- Tell a story: share a story that pulls on people's hearts and shows the direct impact your organization is making. For example, Jason might share a testimonial in which the person explains what it meant to receive interview training and a suit.
- Call to action: tell people exactly what you hope to accomplish and give them a time frame. Be very specific here. A call to action should be clear and concise. For example, "Please help us raise $300 for a Roc Solid Ready Bag."

Another fun way to use social media is birthday fundraisers through Facebook. Encourage people to create a donation page through which people give to your mission in honor of the person's birthday. In one year we raised over $8,000 in birthday donations alone. Many times we didn't ask for people to do this. They chose to support the mission on their own.

SAY THANK YOU

Yes, I sound like a broken record. No matter what kind of fundraising you do—golf tournament, gala, private event, campus tour, digital—don't forget to thank everyone who donates.

Most people and organizations give with no promise of return, so if they receive a thank-you, they take notice. Sending handwritten thank-you notes is a simple way to make your nonprofit stand out.

If you don't have the resources to invest in a donor management system, create an Excel spreadsheet. Include basic info like their name, email, phone, the best way to contact them, and the company they work for. In addition, create a column to keep track of the type of thank-you sent—for example, a handwritten note, a Starbucks gift card, a letter with a photo. This column is important for repeat donors; you don't want to send the same thing over and over. To make thank-yous and future conversations personal, I also include a column for the person's birthday and kids' names.

If you don't have the resources to get branded thank-you cards, go to the dollar store and buy a pack! Then sit down and write a note. This is a sure way to move to the top of the nonprofit leaderboard.

One thing to keep in mind when you use Facebook for social media fundraising is that you do not have access to the people who give money. You get a check or an auto payment in your bank account, but you do not receive any contact information, so you can't follow up for future fundraising campaigns. The good news is that Facebook charges no fees and the fundraising pages are very easy to set up. Simplicity breeds success.

Galas, private events, campus tours, and online fundraising are my top choices, but here's the golden rule behind them all: just ask. Just ask people to join your mission. Ask them to consider a monthly donation. The answer is always no if you don't ask.

At first, directly asking family, friends, and coworkers was very challenging for me. It's a lot easier to invite people to a golf tournament, gala, or private event because they're getting something in return, but these events take a lot of time. I can only speak for myself when I say that I was not called to host golf tournaments. I was called to love and serve kids fighting cancer. In the nonprofit world, it's easy to get distracted by events and forget the simplicity of just asking.

We tend to think of money as something personal. To effectively use the "just ask" technique, you need to throw out that thought and realize that money is a tool to help you accomplish your mission.

Remember: you are not asking for yourself. You are asking for the community you've been called to love and serve. When I ask for a donation, I'm not asking for Eric Newman. I'm asking for Jillian. I'm asking for Allison. I'm asking for Derek. Once you can make that switch, you'll start to overcome the emotional roller coaster of asking people for money.

The answer is always no if you don't ask.

Start by making a list of your inner twenty—the twenty people who believe in *you* first and foremost, because at this point your mission might still be in process. Then get on the phone and call them. Yes, call them. In a world of nonverbal communication, your ask should always be personal.

I was so nervous at first that I would create a lot of small talk and eventually get to, "Well, the reason for my call today is..." Now I get right to it. I'll start with, "Hey, I know we haven't talked for a while, but I just wanted to bring you up to speed on some things I'm doing in the community. Is this a good time to talk?"

Before hanging up, always ask the person if they know anyone else who would be interested in getting involved or giving toward your mission. If they say yes but are hesitant to hand out the person's contact information, tell them you will follow up.

When do you stop following up? When the person tells you to stop. You have no idea what else is going on in their life. They may have simply forgotten. In the last twelve years, I have never had someone knock down my door begging to give money to Roc Solid. You have to follow up. Sometimes it may feel uncomfortable or like you are annoying the person. Maybe you are, but remember you are not asking for yourself; you are asking for the community you were called to love and serve.

For the follow-up process, use a ranking system from one to three, with ones being the really hot leads. After you have followed up two or three times a week for about a month, start following up once every two weeks. If they still don't respond, go to once a month. After that, for us, their name goes into a database, and they'll receive our quarterly newsletter, so they'll still hear from us and be reminded of our mission. As mentioned earlier, you don't have to buy a fancy system to keep track of your contacts and follow-up. Just add a column to the Excel spread-sheet to keep track of when you reach out, whether it is weekly, monthly, or quarterly.

Once you land a meeting, start by getting to know your audience. Ask what's important to them. This will help you navigate the conversation and make your ask more precise. Always do a little homework before the meeting. If the person is a business owner or leader in any capacity, look up the organization's values and use them as a reference point when you connect. This is all part of knowing your audience and speaking their language. For example, if I know the person has three kids who all play soccer, I know they value family and play, which is what Roc Solid values. I might say, "Hey, Jim, you know just as much as I do that your kids come alive when they're on the field. For these kids fighting cancer, the first thing they lose out on is play. We just built a playset for a seven-year-old girl and she's been on it for the last three weeks nonstop. I'm asking if you would consider making a contribution of a hundred bucks so we can do the same for another child."

Bring printed material, but don't give it to the person until the meeting is over. For me, I'm trying to make a personal connection, not a business one. I give my ten-minute pitch, ask them to consider a gift of a specific amount, and then shut up. That last part is the hardest, but I've learned to embrace the awkward silence—and it is awkward—because the next person to speak loses. If you crack under the pressure of the silence, you will start rambling, which will move the conversation away from the ask.

If the person says no, remember they are not saying no to you. People give and choose not to give because of something in themselves. We can come prepared, have the best photos and testimonies, and people will still say no. Don't take it personally. Maybe their business had a bad quarter. Maybe they're going through a divorce. Maybe they recently put their child into an expensive private school. I have learned to make a mental shift: the person might simply mean *not right now*. Also, consider what you could have done differently. Maybe you were off on the amount asked for. Maybe you didn't have their values right. Maybe your mission isn't their mission—that might be the hardest to digest. Not every heart will align with yours, and although you think it should, you can't force it. Move on, and keep your eye on your mission.

IT TAKES MONEY TO MAKE MONEY

In the nonprofit world, there are certain expectations around the amount of money spent on fundraising expenses. My informal research showed that the commonly accepted percentage of income that can be spent on fundraising—the venue, the meal, the technology, and so on—is 5 to 10 percent. That number bugged me because the only way to keep costs down to that level is to have a bake sale or sell cookies outside the grocery store like the Girl Scouts. There's nothing wrong with a bake sale (or the Girl Scouts!), but if you're truly setting out to solve a problem that's bigger than you, a plastic bag of chocolate chip cookies won't cut it.

To change the world, you have to be willing to step out of the bake sale mentality. You have to spend money. Don't go overboard; you have to strike a balance. As the leader of your organization, if you can lay your head down at night knowing the funds you are spending are necessary to give hope to a child fighting cancer, or help a guy living on the street get a job, or repair a couple's credit so they can buy a house, then you're doing your job. Risk equals reward. No matter what you do, there will typically be the people who think you spend too much money on fundraising. Don't let that perception slow you down. Your community deserves better than a baked goods sale.

This is one reason you have a board of directors, including an accountant. They can help you make the best financial decisions for those you love and serve. Your values are also there for you to lean on when you are making decisions like this. Use your values to test the fundraising decisions you're making. I make sure I'm focusing on families first, theirs and ours; that I'm focused on the people, knowing the money will come. The whole reason I spend money to put on fundraisers is because I want the guests to have the best possible experience and to see, feel, and touch our mission. If that happens, they will become storytellers and help push the mission forward.

Feeling the burden of the bake sale mentality doesn't go away. I still wrestle with whether or not to spend money on fundraisers. Then I go back to my values and that allows me to sleep at night. I think about the two thousand Ready Bags we sent out this year. If I had listened to the critics or my own doubts, those two thousand families wouldn't have received that shimmer of light in possibly the darkest moment of their lives.

When your programs are working and lives are being changed, it's easy to become attached to a certain way of doing things. In the next chapter, we'll discuss why it's important to stay married to your mission, not the model.

Chapter 7

MARRY YOUR MISSION, NOT THE MODEL

One Thursday in 2017, we received a call from our local children's hospital. A five-year-old boy was being kept in the hospital longer than necessary because social services considered his home unsafe to live in. Unfortunately, his health insurance did not deem the extended stay at the hospital medically necessary and would not continue to pay for services. The boy basically got evicted and needed to be out by the following Monday.

About five years earlier, we had created a room makeover program in which we surprised mainly older pediatric cancer fighters with a remodeled bedroom. Because they knew about Roc Solid and the program, the hospital called to see if we could help this family. With my construction background, I made a few phone calls and had a team at the house within a few short hours.

My team and I were waiting for the dad when he pulled in the driveway with his twelve-year-old daughter. When they got out of the car, I realized the girl wasn't coming home from school but from work. This honor-roll student had quit school to hang drywall with her dad so they could afford electricity.

Inside the trailer, we learned the dad had been in the middle of a remodel when his five-year-old was diagnosed with cancer. At that point, the mom quit her job so she could stay at the hospital with her son. The family was already strapped for cash, and when the mom had to quit her job, there was no money left to finish the remodel. It was the middle of August. The air conditioner did not work, the home had no insulation, and there were holes in the bathroom floor. The conditions were indeed unsafe, but not because of neglect. The family was trying but could not catch a break.

My team was so touched by this family that they worked around the clock to remodel that boy's bedroom and then moved through the rest of the house to fix as much as possible. They replaced the subfloor and installed new toilets, new vinyl in the kitchen, and even a brand-new heating and cooling system. If they could fix it, they did.

We finished Monday morning, and the boy was able to come home that afternoon. When I handed the keys to the father, tears filled his eyes and he thanked me repeatedly.

Does this sound like a program that isn't working? We brought hope to a child fighting cancer and gave him and his family a safe place to live and play.

Yet we stopped offering the room makeover program four months later.

Why would we do that? That decision certainly didn't come easy, nor did it win us any popularity votes in the community. I received a few angry texts and emails saying we were getting too big and losing our way. Some even accused me of turning my back on part of the pediatric community; that's the dagger that hurt the most.

At that point in 2017, we had three models for accomplishing our mission of bringing hope to every child fighting cancer: Ready Bags, playsets, and room makeovers. The Ready Bags were nonnegotiable. They were the surefire way we could bring hope to every child fighting cancer. They provide light in the family's darkest hour by letting them know they are loved and not alone. We were working toward the goal of giving Ready Bags to every newly diagnosed child across the United States.

The playsets were also a foundational piece of our organization. They solved the problem of lost play, the initial problem that fueled our mission. We had plenty of sponsors and volunteers to help us fund and build hope for kids across the country.

The room makeovers, however, were a different story. Because each remodel was unique, based on the interests of the child, we were consistently hit with unexpected costs in repairs and construction material. In some cases, in the process of making updates, we exposed major safety concerns. For example, we would start to hang a new light fixture and find the wires had been crossed. Because of the potential hazard, we could not put the wires back the way we found them, so we would have to trace the problem to the root and fix it, which sometimes cost thousands of dollars. We also had liability issues with room makeovers. In a few cases our volunteers were accused of taking personal belongings from the house, and a couple of families threatened to sue our organization. Finally, we had a harder time finding sponsors and volunteers since remodeling a room takes a higher degree of construction knowledge. It's one thing to drill a screw into a swing set; it's another thing to replace a floor that has had water damage for several years. Often, these projects called for certified electricians or heating and cooling companies, adding more time and cost.

Bottom line: room makeovers were far from simple, and given our value to Respect Simplicity, we couldn't justify continuing the program. So, with the full agreement of the board, we dropped it. Even though the model was working in many ways, it was also keeping us from fulfilling our mission of bringing hope to every child fighting cancer.

Though it was a gut-wrenching decision, the last two years have shown it was the right one. Instead of delivering 110 Ready Bags a year, we have been able to send out 2,000.

Marrying your mission, not your model, means you stay dedicated to the reason for your existence and are willing to change the programs that are keeping you from accomplishing it—even if the programs appear to be working in the short term.

Change is hard and often scary, but it is often necessary to stay focused on your purpose. In this chapter we'll look at what it means to stay married to your mission and how you can continually evaluate what's working so you can best help the community you've been called to love and serve.

MISSION VS. MODEL

The mission of any nonprofit is the reason it exists. It

points to the problem you're trying to solve for a specific community. The mission of Roc Solid Foundation, for example, is to build hope for every child fighting pediatric cancer. That's our sole purpose, and it came about because I lost two cousins to pediatric cancer and I know firsthand how hopeless that situation can be.

The model of any nonprofit is how they go about accomplishing their mission. Roc Solid has a two-part model: we deliver Ready Bags and we build playsets.

As your organization grows and changes, you will likely see the need to change your model. Staying married to your mission instead of your model allows you the "rigid flexibility" to make those shifts so you can stay dedicated to loving and serving your community at all costs. It's what allowed us to stop doing room makeovers when it became clear that we could use the resources to serve more children.

The mission of cancer research, for example, is to cure cancer, but doctors and scientists keep changing their model to find new treatments that provide the cure. If one drug doesn't work, they don't drop the mission of curing cancer. They simply change the model and look for another way to cure this horrible disease.

The problem is that when the mission is being accomplished using a certain program, we can easily become married to the model of that specific program and refuse to change even when it's no longer the best way to serve the community. Any change is hard, even changing for the better, but it's necessary. If you marry the mission, you'll do whatever it takes to see it accomplished. It becomes the anchor that keeps you from drifting. If you marry the model, however, you might make decisions that drift from your purpose and ultimately don't serve your community.

HOW TO STAY MARRIED TO THE MISSION

It's hard to tell if you're becoming too attached to your model. Here are some suggestions for making sure that doesn't happen.

"IT'S ALWAYS BEEN DONE THIS WAY"

Those words are a death sentence for any nonprofit, business, or organization. Watch for this thinking in yourself and in your volunteers, staff, and board of directors. Run from this phrase like a giant brown bear is chasing you. Once you get away from it, turn around and see who has kept up with you. Those are the people who will help you take your organization to the next level and change when the time comes. It's easy to get caught up in where you've been and not where you're going.

Unfortunately, your original launch team can be the biggest hindrance to changing the model. The launch team is the group of people who helped you bring your vision into reality. They showed up early and stayed up late. They poured blood, sweat, and tears into creating the programs that brought the mission to life.

Because they are so invested, however, your launch team can become married to the model they helped create. If members of your original crew are saying, "But it's always been done this way," it's time to have some hard conversations. You can make these chats a little easier by sharing the upcoming change prior to actually making it. Cast a clear vision of why the change is needed and let people share feedback. Ultimately, however, if you and your board know the change is for the best, you can't let these opposing voices sway you from doing what's necessary. If you do, your organization can easily become stagnant and, worse, stop fulfilling its purpose. Mission trumps opinion every time.

Do not be afraid to lose the people. If you do, know that you are not alone. In the twelve years of Roc Solid Foundation, three things have been around from the beginning: me, my wife, and kids fighting cancer. People have left for various reasons, including a stalemate over a model that needed to change as we grew. It happens. People will come and go, but remember: you have overcome much worse, and your community is counting on you.

Mission trumps opinion every time.

NUMBERS DON'T LIE

Pay attention to the numbers in your programs and activities. I don't think numbers paint the whole picture, but they do fill in some details that make the painting come to life. In particular, you want to look at trends. How many volunteers are showing up? If that number is decreasing, it's worth figuring out why. How much does each project cost? Are you consistently going over budget? How many people are you reaching with the money that you have been gifted? If you are consistently over budget and the number of people you're able to reach is decreasing, it's probably time to reevaluate the effectiveness of the model.

One of the guiding numbers at Roc Solid Foundation is 16,000. Our goal is to put 16,000 Ready Bags into the hands of families who have just heard the worst news of their life. Why 16,000? Because, depending on which study you read, 16,000 children are diagnosed with cancer each year in the United States, and our mission is to bring hope to *every* child fighting cancer. At the time we decided to drop the room makeovers, we were at less than half a percent of reaching that goal. I was not okay with that. If we would have continued down the same path without changing our programs, it would have taken us seventy-five years to hit 16,000. Now we're at 12.4 percent of our goal, and we're on track to reach our goal of 16,000 Ready Bags in less than eight years. Once we are able to reach the US goal, then we can start looking at a global footprint to love and serve *every* child with cancer.

FEEDBACK IS YOUR FRIEND

If numbers suggest a program isn't working, investigate further. Ask your customers what they think. You need to find out if you're spinning your wheels to create resources for something that isn't actually accomplishing your mission.

After our build, we will sometimes call the people we served to get feedback. We usually wait a couple weeks, until the rainbows and unicorns of the experience have fallen to the ground and they've had time to think about how we helped them and what we could have done better. The second part is particularly key. If you constantly focus on what can be improved, you already have a mindset toward potentially changing the model if it's not working best for the community you're serving. For example, if you delivered twenty-five food boxes to families that needed Thanksgiving dinner, follow up with questions like, "Was the food fresh? Did we provide you with everything needed? How was your volunteer interaction? What can we improve on next to better love and serve you?" Feedback is all about getting better, and getting better might mean changing your model.

HAVE THE HARD CONVERSATION

The hard conversation starts with you. You have to be willing to consider that the current model isn't working or isn't the best way to move your mission forward.

People have called me a "pioneer of change." I used to think that was awesome, until I remembered that pioneers get shot, lost in the wilderness, or beaten as they forge a path for others. To do what's best for those you serve, you have to be willing to take the bullets, the punches, and being misunderstood. That might mean having hard conversations and making unpopular decisions with people who are hanging on to models that are no longer best serving the mission.

When you consider changing programs, you're going to hear the most bickering and complaining from the people married to your model—those people sitting in "high chairs," off to the side of the main table, who are making a racket, just like a crying baby. If you turn to take care of the noisy high-chair people, you turn your back on the people at the table, the people who catch the vision and are dedicated to the mission, not just the model. Not a smart use of time. I choose to suck it up and have the hard conversation so those high-chair people either get on board or leave. If they decide to leave, so be it. It's hard, but remember, it happens.

CONDUCT AN ANNUAL EVALUATION

In addition to your more frequent requests for feedback from your community, take time once a year to evaluate. I look at evaluations as doing maintenance on a car. If you take your car into the shop on a regular basis, you are taking steps to avoid a breakdown. If you refuse to do scheduled maintenance, when your car does break down, it will likely cost you more money and require more repairs. As the leader of the organization, take time to schedule a maintenance evaluation to avoid breakdowns.

Here are a few questions to get you started:

- What parts of your model are working?
- What is the best-case scenario if the model continues working?
- What is the worst-case scenario if it doesn't?
- One year from now, what does your model look like if you choose not to change?

Somewhere in the answers to these questions lies the next step for your organization.

For this annual evaluation, I bring in the chairperson of the board and two or three other people who have influence—for example, people who have volunteered at builds or otherwise seen the model in action. I make sure these people are not yes-men. To make sure we're truly evaluating if programs are working, I need people who are honest.

If you wait for perfection, you'll never move.

During this meeting, evaluate the model (or models) and ask if it is still pointing to the mission. If so, why is it working? If it's not working, why not? Then decide what to do to make sure you stay married to the mission. Does that mean tweaking a program? Getting rid of it altogether?

You likely won't be able to change everything, so here's another opportunity to prioritize with your ones, twos, and threes. Then create an action plan. Don't aim for perfection. If you wait for perfection, you'll never move. Instead, aim for a stronger united purpose among your staff and volunteers.

EVALUATE COMBUSTION POINTS

In addition to an annual evaluation, constantly be on the lookout for potential combustion points, or places where you're most likely to run into the worst-case scenario. Combustion points have the potential to cause an explosion within your organization, slowing down or completely derailing your mission, at least temporarily.

In Roc Solid, one combustion point was that we couldn't find enough key leaders to travel to the sites and host the playset builds all over the United States. This was happening before the pandemic, but COVID made it clear we needed to change our model to keep up with the demand for playsets.

Pre-pandemic, we deployed Roc Solid teams to build playsets in different locations around the United States, and we sold the experience to corporate America as a team-building exercise. With COVID, most of the corporate team-building events we sold got canceled. That's a lot of kids who weren't going to get playsets.

The world was shutting down around us, but cancer didn't stop, so we quickly changed our model. Instead of having teams from corporate America building hope, we started Roc Solid on Demand (ROD) and deployed the playsets straight to the families in need, and then the families themselves, along with friends, built them. At the same time, we realized we needed to transition from being experts at building the playsets to being experts at teaching others how to build them. Along with the playset pieces, we provided how-to videos, not only for assembling the actual playset but also for creating the same experience that our Roc Solid teams did. We sent T-shirts, we encouraged them to buy pizza, and we even included a blindfold to put on the child before the playset was revealed.

Don't let the model become a roadblock just because it paved the way to where you are currently standing.

As a result of this shift, we actually increased the number of playsets built in a year. With our usual corporate team-building model in place, we were scheduled to build seventy-five to one hundred playsets in 2020. After we shifted to ROD, we were able to build two hundred play-sets in *one month*, and we closed out the year at a total of three hundred. That growth wouldn't have been possible if we had stayed married to the model. Play defeated cancer, even in the midst of a pandemic.

In addition, this shift has changed the trajectory of our organization going forward. The team-building model is now called Play It Forward, and we are scheduled to build seventy-five playsets in 2021 through our original program. In addition, we have four hundred builds scheduled under the new ROD model.

Don't let the model become a roadblock just because it

paved the way to where you are currently standing. It used to take three to four Roc Solid team members to oversee one hundred projects through the year. Now it takes two people to complete four hundred playsets. We have been able to scale, not for the sake of scaling but to better complete our mission.

EXPECT A RIPPLE EFFECT

The year after we stopped doing room makeovers, our Ready Bag program grew by 100 percent, and it grew another 100 percent the year after that. Yes, I took the shots, read the nasty emails, and endured many coffee meetings where people expressed their extreme disappointment in me. With the support of my board of directors and other key contributors, I made an unpopular decision, one that created more opportunities for us to accomplish our mission. That sometimes happens when you marry the mission and those around you are stuck married to the model.

When you choose to change the model in favor of staying married to the mission, there will be a ripple effect. People may not understand. They may stop volunteering or giving money. That is a tough pill to swallow, but it's okay. The longer you prolong making that hard decision, however, the bigger the ripples will be—the more money you'll waste on things that don't best support your mission, the more people will support the current model and then react when it begins to shift. That's why it's important to act quickly when you see the model needs to be changed, when you've reached a combustion point. There will always be a ripple effect, but you can minimize it if you are constantly evaluating your model and act swiftly when you realize it's no longer working.

Knowing any shift made will cause a ripple effect, we've developed a plan to prepare for it. We call a staff meeting and we sit down to identify the ripples we will likely experience in people, culture, and funding. For example, when we decided to drop the room makeovers, we talked to the people who would be most affected by the decision—the designers and key leaders—and explained the vision for the change and offered an ear to their concerns. We also took steps to manage the culture on our build sites, to discourage negative talk about the room makeover decision. Finally, we identified the donors who were specifically giving to the room makeover program and talked to them individually, before the decision went public. All but 15 percent decided to shift their donation to another Roc Solid program. If we hadn't called, we could have lost about $30,000 a year in donations.

Over the years, I have had many key volunteers refuse to buy into the new direction of the organization because they loved the old model. I had to have hard conversations with them, knowing that they might leave. It's never easy to lose established volunteers, but if they can't support a new model or the idea of change, your mission may not be what is best for them at this time. Hanging on will only hurt the organization and the community you love and serve.

MISSION CREEP

When an organization is successful in one area, there's a tendency to think, *Oh, I'm gaining momentum. Let me try this and this and this!* I'm guilty of it, just like everyone else.

We started Roc Solid with playsets and then added Ready Bags. When I saw those were going well, I started adding other programs, like a date night for the parents stuck at the hospital with their child fighting cancer. We arranged for someone to sit with the child at the hospital and hired a limo to pick up the parents and take them to a fancy restaurant for dinner. Parents loved it, but that model veered away from our true purpose of bringing hope to *every* child fighting cancer. That's mission creep: doing something just because you can, even though it might cause you to "creep" past your original mission.

Around the time we were deciding whether to continue

the room makeovers, I traveled to New Orleans for a speaking gig. I had a little extra time, so I went to the famous Café Du Monde.

I arrived minutes after it opened, so the café was nearly empty. I sat down at one of the tables, and an older woman asked me what I wanted.

"I haven't been given a menu," I said.

She pointed to the napkin holder, which had one drink choice and one food choice: coffee and beignets. I asked for one of each, and a few minutes later, she returned with my order.

The coffee was the perfect temperature. It was hands down one of the best coffees I've ever tasted. The beignets were perfection. Café Du Monde were experts in two things: coffee and beignets. They didn't try to get fancy or add new things to the menu just because they could. They kept it simple, and yet they were known around the world.

Right there in the café, I realized doing room makeovers was like selling donuts when I'm an expert in beignets. It was a powerful illustration of mission creep that I ultimately shared with my board when I pitched the idea of changing our model.

By the time I finished my coffee and beignets, a line of customers had wrapped around the whole building. I looked across the street, where there was a café with a sign that read, "We have beignets too!" Five hundred things on their menu, including beignets, and no one was waiting to get in.

I get calls from the American Heart Association, the Down Syndrome Society, and other organizations wanting us to build playsets for the children they serve. My answer is always no, because if I say yes to them, I say no to a child fighting cancer, and that's the community I was called to love and serve. Jason gets calls from people asking him to provide suits and interview training for college grads. His answer is always no, because he was called to love and serve men struggling with homelessness, not college grads. Mission creep stops you from becoming an expert in carrying out your purpose because you're always chasing the shiny new thing. You'll get a lot faster if you stay in your lane.

Just because you can doesn't mean you should.

As your organization grows and as your mission comes to life, make sure you stay anchored to your purpose. I would love to tell you that staying married to the mission is easy, but it's not. The more success you encounter, the more people will buy into what you're doing, but with more people comes more opinions. As the number of opinions that carry weight increases, so does the risk of becoming married to the model instead of the mission. Make sure you're deeply rooted in who you're serving and why.

So far we have focused on all the different aspects of your nonprofit. Now we're going to talk about you.

Chapter 8

WHO YOU BECOME IS MORE IMPORTANT THAN WHAT YOU DO

As Roc Solid Foundation grew, I found myself at a cap in terms of knowledge. I'm a contractor—I can pour concrete and I can frame a house. I had gotten the organization this far, but I was stumped on how to keep moving forward. I needed help. I needed someone with experience and wisdom. I needed a mentor.

At the same time, I wanted to be more than a great CEO. I wanted to be a leader who valued the people who showed up to work every day. I wanted to learn how to be successful without sacrificing my relationship with my wife and kids. In short, I wanted to find someone who could teach me how to make the best decisions, build a successful organization, and not lose my faith and family in the process.

I went back to my journal and wrote down the names of people who fit this description, and I identified one possible mentor from my Thursday morning Bible study. John showed up every week in camouflage bedroom slippers, holey jeans, a stained T-shirt, and a baseball cap sitting crooked on his head. He had recently retired from his position as the head of a multimillion-dollar food distribution company, yet he was the furthest thing from what I thought a CEO should look like. He was also a man of faith. I was very intrigued, so I researched John's track record and found out he was an extremely competent and successful leader, so I asked him to coffee, with hopes of him agreeing to become my mentor.

I spent two weeks preparing for our first meeting. I gathered charts, budgets, spreadsheets, graphs—all the documents I thought a CEO should have. I arrived fifteen minutes early. I even dressed in a fancy suit, one that actually fit me this time.

John walked in wearing boat shoes and his usual holey jeans, T-shirt, and crooked cap.

As soon as he sat down, I dove right into my rehearsed agenda and didn't stop for the next thirty minutes. Finally, John held up his hand and took the longest, most drawn-out sip of coffee I've ever seen. Then he picked up my folder and tossed it to the side.

"Listen," John said after setting all of my hard work aside. "I'm not worried about that stuff. You'll have people to help you with that. I'm more concerned about who you are than what you'll ever do."

I was speechless. I was trying to figure out how to respond, but I couldn't find the words. John continued. "I've been praying a lot about this. If you want to do this mentoring thing, this is what's going to happen. For every ten times we meet, we're going to spend one meeting talking business. The other times I want to talk about Eric Newman, the husband and father. I'm going to find out how your wife and kids are doing. If you can get that right, then you'll be the CEO that this company needs.

"The truth is that when you leave this organization, they're going to replace you. At best, they'll have an oil painting of you that will scare most people while it hangs on the wall and collects dust. Who you are is more important than what you do."

That last statement changed everything for me. I was still a little confused about the oil painting, but I knew John was the right guy to have in my life. I showed up the next Tuesday morning and every Tuesday after that for the next three and a half years. Who I have become as a CEO, and more importantly, as a husband and father, is because of what I learned from John.

In this chapter we'll look at how to keep your priorities straight so that you keep your focus on who you're becoming and not what you're doing. Your organization and personal life will both benefit as a result.

Who you are is more important than what you do.

DEALING WITH FOUNDER'S SYNDROME

When I first met with John, I was very much caught up in what *I* was doing for Roc Solid Foundation. I said all the right things about who we were serving and boasted about how great our mission was. In reality, I was really starring in the Eric Newman Show. Though I may not have said so, I truly believed Roc Solid would fall apart without me. That's the essence of founder's syndrome.

When you pour your heart and soul into bringing a vision to reality, it's easy to think you are the only reason it's working. After all, you're the Chief Everything Officer, right? In many ways you do carry it all on your shoulders, at least in the beginning.

And let's be honest, being in the spotlight is addictive. Receiving all those accolades for what you're doing feels amazing. The problem is that you start believing that you really did make it happen all on your own. In reality, it has taken a community, but founder's syndrome keeps you from giving other people credit for their part in building the program and accomplishing the mission.

Here's the hard truth I learned from John: if you want your organization to continue after you're gone, you need to move beyond doing it all. You need to learn to let go and teach others to lead so that when you're gone, your nonprofit will continue to carry out its mission. Being the Chief Everything Officer is not sustainable. No one can do everything. The worst part is that if you continue carrying it all on your shoulders, they'll eventually get weak and you may find yourself buried underneath the rubble of all your blood, sweat, and tears.

Founder's syndrome happens when you cannot get out of your own way. If you're building something valuable and sustainable, then your goal should be to create something that will operate without you. You won't be able to accomplish that if you can't put your pride aside and get out of your own way.

How can you tell if you're struggling with founder's syndrome? One way is to look at your organization's social media posts. How many pictures feature you, instead of the community you're serving? How many of your posts include the word *I* instead of *we*? Been there, done that. Guilty as charged.

Here are a few suggestions for kicking founder's syndrome to the curb once and for all.

LET GO AND DELEGATE

First and foremost, you have to learn to let go. This was one of my biggest struggles. Even though I worked alongside amazing and dedicated people, I had a hard time acknowledging that they were capable of handling tasks I'd been doing. I came to understand they might not do it exactly like I would, but they could do it, and I needed to let them.

Letting go involves delegating. This means trusting your team and the process you have in place. As with letting go, I also struggled with delegation. I started by asking people one simple question: "Can you help me with this?" Then I made sure I painted a clear picture of what I was asking of them. I quickly learned that delegation requires details. When you give someone a task, you can't assume they'll know exactly what you're thinking and how you want it done. If you want something done a certain way, you need to spell out those expectations. Otherwise you'll end up giving people a blank canvas and wonder why they didn't paint the masterpiece you saw in your head.

When you start delegating, you might find that people come to you because they don't know what to do, or perhaps they're scared to make the wrong move. In an effort to let go and empower my team at the same time, I would simply say, "You decide." For a while, I told people I would only make decisions on Thursdays. "If you can wait until Thursday, great. If not, you decide."

When you delegate, don't just hand off the tasks you don't want to do. Delegate the good stuff, too. I like to speak at events, but so do some of my staff and key volunteers. Why not give them the chance to shine? It used to be that people wouldn't give money if I weren't at the fundraisers, but as we grew, I couldn't be everywhere. I had to train people to share our story. I had to delegate. As a result, my team members have become more visible, and I have started staying behind the scenes. As I learned, you become less, and they become more.

The power is in the decision. If you decide not to delegate—if you decide that you can't trust your team or your process—that will be the defining moment for your organization. Your mission will hit a wall because there's only so much you alone can do. You will eventually run out of steam. You have the power to choose. Make the decision. Delegate.

You become less, and they become more.

Delegation does not mean you take your hands off the wheel completely. As the founder of the organization, the buck ultimately stops with you, so you still want to make sure things are getting done and running smoothly.

To help with this, I use the 10-80-10 rule when I delegate: for anything deemed major, I'm there for the first 10 percent to set the vision, communicate expectations, and set the direction. I call this the launch. Then I delegate 80 percent of the responsibility to the team. That's the flying time, when people might experience turbulence but it's usually not life-threatening. As the leader, you have to let the turbulence happen and allow the team to grow from it. Remember, you're planning for the day when you're no longer there. Then I come in for the last 10 percent and help the plane. This model has been a game changer for me and my team.

When I delegate something, I also put a time limit on when it should be done. You can't assume the person knows what's going on inside your head, so spell it out.

I also have people repeat back to me what I asked them to do, not because I question their intelligence, but because we tend to hear things differently (bonus marital advice right there!). Doing this clears any gray areas or misinterpretation of what is expected of them.

The reason I failed at delegating during my first four years is that I didn't think anyone could do it better than me. Not only was that disrespectful to my team, it was also disrespectful to the kids fighting cancer because my pride stunted the organization's growth. As part of my own professional development, I started studying a different topic every quarter, and delegation was one of them. If you find yourself struggling with letting go and delegating, check out *Art of Delegation* by Charles Malone or *What Got You Here Won't Get You There* by Marshall Goldsmith. You could spend the rest of your life trying to master the art of delegation. These two books are a place to start.

The same principle applies to delegating as in fundraising: *the answer is always no if you don't ask.* People want to help, but you have to ask.

SOMETHING HAD TO GIVE

In 2017 the organization was flourishing, but I was drained. Even though I had made some progress in delegating, in many ways, I was still functioning as the Chief Everything Officer. I had spent so much time pouring into everyone else, but I had not filled my own tank.

Heart work is hard work.

The last straw was attending a funeral for one of the kids we had built a playset for. I finally got to the point where I had nothing else to give, and I was ready to quit. I even got as far as drafting a resignation letter, but before I turned it in, I visited a pastor friend who shared advice that saved me from myself: "Eric, if you're quitting because it's hard, you're going to regret it the rest of your life."

After I tore up the letter, I went to the board of directors and told them I needed some time to invest in myself and my family. My assistant suggested that I take a six-week sabbatical, completely disconnected from Roc Solid. I wrestled with that idea for a long time because I still thought the wheels would fall off the organization without me in the driver's seat. When I told my buddy what I was thinking, he said, "Well, you were just thinking about quitting. What did you think would happen if you were gone permanently?"

Good point. So, I turned in my cell phone, changed my email, and disappeared with my family for six weeks. The only person who knew how to get in touch with me was my assistant, but she didn't.

That sabbatical saved me. During that time, I truly learned how to let go, to trust my team and our process. When I came back, my team was a whole new team. When I wasn't there, they were forced to make decisions. They had to get better. When the people around you become better, they don't need you as much—which is a good thing, even though it feels a little like being put out to pasture sometimes.

If you've poured your heart and soul into your mission like I know you have, you will likely get to the point where you're done. Please remember that quitting when it gets hard is not the answer. You'll regret it for the rest of your life. Thank God I had people around to prevent me from making that mistake. They cared more about who I was than what I did. Surround yourself with people like that. Heart work is hard work. Take time to invest in yourself and your family; those are your true priorities.

KEEP YOUR PRIORITIES STRAIGHT

In my office, I have a photo of two white rocking chairs as a reminder of what I'm aiming for: my wife sitting beside me at the end of this journey. When I've left Roc Solid in someone else's capable hands and my kids are grown, I'll be spending the rest of my days with the person who matters most. That photo reminds me to keep my priorities straight now so I don't miss out on an amazing future.

YOUR UNIQUES

As a founder, it's easy to get caught in the comparison

game, but comparison is a game you will always lose, especially if you're comparing your first year to another founder's tenth year. Comparison can lead you to chase the new and shiny things, which can lead to mission creep and marrying the model instead of the mission. Comparison can cause you to push, push, push—but you often push the right things out of the way and focus on the wrong things.

When we compare, we lose sight of the things that are uniquely ours, the few things that make each one of us truly, well, unique: our faith, our significant other, and our children. When John shared this thought with me in one of our meetings, he said many people focus on their career and neglect their uniqueness. As a result, when they finally retire, they no longer have their uniques because they've been neglecting them for years.

As much as I love kids fighting cancer and my Roc Solid team, who do I want around me when this life is coming to an end and I am on my deathbed? Do I want a bunch of lawyers and social media cameras or even my board of directors, as wonderful as they are? No. I want my wife and kids. I want those two white rocking chairs facing the ocean, one for me and one for my bride.

Identifying my uniques gave me a new focus and aim. I started investing in my family first and foremost, and I also started investing in my team. I became less so they could become more. I also encouraged my staff and volunteers to find their uniqueness and keep their priorities straight. When we're all focusing on our uniques, we are better able to love and serve kids fighting pediatric cancer.

THE PROBLEM TREE

I once read a story about a man who worked in construction. One day his car broke down, and the man's boss gave him a ride home. The man invited his boss inside, and as they walked in the front door, the man rubbed the leaves of a worn-looking plant sitting outside.

The boss asked, "What's that?"

"Oh, that's my problem tree. I leave all my problems from work right there, and I pick up the responsibilities that wait for me inside. When I leave in the morning, I leave the home responsibilities and pick up the work problems."

After my six-week sabbatical, I created my own version of the problem tree. Every day I enter and exit my house through the garage. On a corner next to the steps, I stuck two pieces of duct tape. On the piece that faces the garage, I wrote, "Daddy, Tickle Monster, and Best Husband Ever."

I touch that tape every day after work, before I walk into the house. Sometimes I have to tap it a few times and add a prayer so I can leave my work problems out of the house, and pick up the role my family needs me to be.

In my house, I'm not the CEO. I'm not the founder of Roc Solid. I'm Daddy, Tickle Monster, and Best Husband Ever. Touching that piece of duct tape symbolizes my intention to leave all the work chaos outside and take up the chaos that awaits inside: kids flying into my arms and yelling, "Daddy!"

I can't ignore the work chaos. Ultimately, it stops with me. But I can leave it outside and pick it up the next morning. So, when I leave the house each day, I rub the other piece of tape, the one that faces the house. It says, "Hope." At that point, it's game on, and I'm ready to tackle the chaos at work.

The pieces of tape show which direction takes more work. The Hope side is sharp and easy to read; all I have to do is touch it and I pick up where I left off the night before. The Daddy, Tickle Monster, and Best Husband Ever side is worn out. You can barely read the writing because I have to rub the hell out of it so I can leave those work problems outside the house. I don't get it right every time. Sometimes work consumes me and I have to go back out to the garage and reenter. The great thing is that each day I get to choose who I want to be when I get home, just as much as I get to choose who I want to be when I start my workday. You get the same choice, so choose wisely.

OIL PAINTING OR ROCKING CHAIRS

Don't lose yourself in all the good you're doing. Your kids and your spouse won't care how many suits you donate, how many people you help buy a house, how many Lego sets you provide, or how many playsets you build if you are not putting that same time and effort into them. Instead, they could begin to resent all the good you are doing. Find out what's unique to you, what you really want when your journey with this organization is done, and make decisions today with that in mind.

The fact is that one day, we'll all step away from what we've created. At best they'll give us rubber chicken or seafood at our retirement party. Then they'll have someone create an oil painting and hang it in the boardroom, where it will scare people and collect dust. If that's what you want to dedicate your life to and then end up with an empty home because you didn't prioritize your family, go for it. But what if there's a way to have the rubber chicken, the oil painting, *and* still have your spouse and family waiting for you? What if there is a way to lead this organization with integrity *and* not lose your soul? You'll still end up with the oil painting, but more importantly, you end up with the two rocking chairs.

If we don't know our uniqueness, we may end up with an oil painting in a boardroom and no one sitting beside us in a rocking chair. As much as I love the community I'm called to love and serve, I'm not willing to take that risk. Are you?

CONCLUSION

If you're feeling a bit overwhelmed as you come to the end of this book, that's probably a good sign. It means you're truly tackling something big, much bigger than yourself. Using your pain to fuel your purpose is a road most people don't even consider much less travel, but you are. I've given you the map; now it's time for your road trip.

CHECKLIST

Pull out that journal. It's time to get to work.

The first step is figuring out where you are in the process of starting this nonprofit or business. I've compiled a list of tasks pulled from the chapters of this book. Look it over, figure out where to begin, and start working through them one at a time. Remember, if you get stuck, Google is your friend.

- [ ] Brain dump ideas, questions, fears, and emotions related to your pain point.
- [ ] Identify the problem you are trying to solve.
- [ ] Brainstorm solutions until you land on the solution you wish you had when you were going through the painful situation.
- [ ] Put a "why" photo in your journal.
- [ ] Create your first to-do list and prioritize using ones, twos, and threes.
- [ ] Make a list of potential candidates for your board of directors and start approaching them.
- [ ] Ask a lawyer to help you file the necessary paperwork.
- [ ] Ask an accountant to help you set up a budget and financial statements.
- [ ] Write, polish, and practice your elevator pitch.
- [ ] Write and refine at least one power statement.
- [ ] Design the who, what, when, where, why of your program.
- [ ] Test the program hard and pivot often.
- [ ] Create your values, personal first and then the organization's.
- [ ] Start recruiting volunteers.
- [ ] Start thinking of ways to thank those volunteers.
- [ ] Brainstorm ideas for creative, unique fundraising events that bring guests into your story.
- [ ] Create your inner twenty list and start connecting and calling to share what you're doing and to ask for their financial support.

☐ Find a mentor who shares your values and can help you remember that who you are is more important than what you do.
☐ And above all, remember to ask. The answer is always no if you don't ask.

When (not if) you become overwhelmed at some point along the way, pause, grab your journal, and do a brain dump. Get it all out on the page. Then drop things into buckets and prioritize: ones, twos, threes. Delegate what you can, and get back to work. Brain dump, bucket, prioritize, get to work. Repeat.

When you're tired and wondering if it's all worth it, look at your 'why photo.' Remind yourself that you're not doing all of this for you. You're doing it for the community you've been called to love and serve. You're doing it because the pain you've gone through has put you in a unique position to help others.

THE REAL STORY

Early on, we had another build in the pouring rain. I again tried to cancel it because the rain was coming in from all directions. This time, however, my decision was not based on fear but on my concern for the safety of our team and the volunteers.

The problem was that the sponsor worked really hard to get a professional athlete and the press to join us, so they begged us not to cancel. We were supposed to do four or five projects that day, but because the weather was so bad, I had already sent the teams home. After confirming that the athlete was on his way, I called everyone back, half expecting them not to turn around since they were already thirty minutes into their drive home.

Every single team member came back—not for the professional athlete, but for Gabrielle, the beautiful little girl fighting cancer.

We arrived at the site and tried to set up, but the wind kept blowing things over. After we finally staked everything down, we started building. It was cold and wet and miserable, two and half hours of pure hell.

The sponsor finally arrived and set up tents, followed by the professional athlete in his gleaming white sneakers, trying in vain to float across the water.

After we finished building, the local news station asked me for an interview. As I spoke, water dripped off the hood of my poncho into my face. Suddenly, the publicist tapped the news reporter on the shoulder, and said, "Hey, he's not the story." Then he turned and pointed to the dry athlete sitting under the tent. "He's the story!"

The publicist was right. I wasn't the story. But that professional athlete wasn't either. The people who built that playset in the rain to give Gabrielle hope and the ability to play—they were the story. The donors who made it possible, our incredible staff, and above all, little Gabrielle—they were the story.

No matter what your pain point or solution, no matter what roadblocks and challenges appear, never lose sight of the true story: the people who have helped you bring your vision into reality and the community you were called to love and serve.

This journey to starting a nonprofit or business with a mission will have its rough spots, but if you've already come through what you have, you can do anything. If a guy who lost everything in a construction company, a guy whose biggest ambition was to surf all over the world, can start a nonprofit with negative $750 in his bank account, so can you. It's not easy, but it's always worth it.

ABOUT THE AUTHOR

ERIC NEWMAN is a passionate entrepreneur, speaker, and visionary leader. In 2009, he founded Roc Solid, an organization that inspires hope for every child and family fighting pediatric cancer. Roc Solid partners with more than seventy children's hospitals to deliver Ready Bags for families and has built more than one thousand playsets for children throughout the country who need a safe place to play and a reason to smile. A husband, father, and pediatric cancer survivor himself, Eric understands the battle a family faces when their child is diagnosed.

Made in the USA
Middletown, DE
28 May 2022

66363933R00135